SHORT STORIES FROM THE HISTORY OF INDIAN ARMY SINCE AUGUST 1947

SHORT STORIES FROM THE HISTORY OF INDIAN ARMY SINCE AUGUST 1947

by

J Francis

Vij Books India Pvt Ltd
New Delhi (India)

Vij Books India Pvt Ltd
(Publishers, Distributors & Importers)
2/19 (Second Floor), Ansari Road, Darya Ganj
New Delhi - 110002
Phones: 91-11-43596460, 91-11- 65449971
Fax: 91-11-47340674
web: www.vijbooks.com
e-mail : vijbooks@rediffmail.com

Copyright © 2013, Author

ISBN: 978-93-82652-17-5

All rights reserved

No part of this book may be reproduced, stored in a retrieval systems, transmitted or utilised in any form or by any means, electronic, mechanical, photocopying, recording or otherwise, without the prior permission of the copyright owner. Application for such permission should be addressed to the publisher.

The views expressed in the book are of the author.

This book is meant for educational and learning purposes, the author of the book has taken all reasonable care to ensure that the contents of the book do not violate any existing copyright or other intellectual property rights of any person in any manner whatsoever. In the event the editor has been unable to track any source and if any copyright has been inadvertently infringed, please notify the publisher in writing for the corrective action.

CONTENTS

Title	Page Number
Foreword	viii
Preface	x
Acknowledgement	xv

1. The First Commanding Officer — 1
2. Saviors of Heaven on Earth - Gallants Galore — 5
3. Pratham Param Vir — 10
4. The Saviors of Naushera — 13
5. Lion of Naushera — 17
6. The Gateway to Ladakh — 20
7. Thapa the Tenacious — 25
8. The Teenage Hero — 30
9. Prelude to 1962 War — 35
10. Winner at the Battle of Chushul — 37
11. Namka Chu The Killing Ground — 45
12. Tawang to Bomdi La — 50
13. Sentinels of Walong — 56
14. Pakistan's Failed Second Kashmir War — 59

15. Fortune Favors the Bold	62
16. Akhnoor Was Threatened	67
17. March to Lahore	70
18. War of Liberation	78
19. Unique Param Vir - Albert	82
20. Hoshiar Singh at Basantar	84
21. Shaheed Arun Khetarpal	87
22. In the words of a Pakistani Brigadier	89
23. Many Firsts Greater Glory	90
24. A String of Barbed wire	92
25. Siachen - Just in Time	98
26. The Fourth Attempt at Kargil	103
27. A Brave Heart	114
28. Peacekeeping Operations	118
29. Kipper and Sam The History Makers	119

Praise for the Book

As the Commandant of Officers Training Academy, Chennai, my task is not only to provide quality pre-commission training to selected young men and women, but also to motivate them to give of their best during their service to the Army and the Nation. I am, therefore, constantly on the lookout for ideas and inspirational inputs which will help our young officers to remain focused and motivated at all times to act and react in an exemplary manner during conflict and crisis situations. Mission-oriented decision making capability will always assist them to galvanize their resources to successfully address the daunting challenges of leadership and motivation in the face of instability and extreme danger.

It is in this context that I found the Book **'Short Stories From The History of Indian Army Since August 1947'**, conceived and compiled by Col J Francis to be interesting and awe inspiring. The short story format of the book, its simple narration style, appropriate profiles and relevant maps will certainly appeal to all young officers and goad them on to pursue a more comprehensive study of our rich military heritage which will stand them in good stead in the pursuit of excellence in their chosen profession.

I commend Col Francis for his path breaking creation and have no hesitation in recommending the book to all those interested in military history and research.

Lt. Gen. S S Jog SM, VSM
Commandant Officers Training Academy, Chennai.

Conquer the fear of death and enjoy living.
Let not the fear of death challenge your life
and make it dreadful.

FOREWORD

Military History has been the subject of many books. These deal with the Art and Science of War. Wars, campaigns and battles are covered at some length in our military literature. Sadly there are very few books or even chapters in these books which focus on the fighting soldier the warrior and his contribution towards achieving the aim of the fighting. Colonel J. Francis has magnificently filled this gap with this book.

This book is presented in the form of fast-paced self-contained stories of bitterly fought actions in which the soldier emerges as the hero. It is his courage, determination, ingenuity and never-say-die spirit that tipped the balance in our favour in most of these actions. In many of these, he was killed in action or later succumbed to his injuries. However, whether he lived or not, his actions on that fateful day helped hold aloft, in honour, the tricolor. Colonel Francis has narrated all this in his simple, direct style, keeping the focus on the soldier and avoiding distracting details. This book has, therefore, turned out to be truly inspirational and 'un-put-down-able'.

I strongly urge everyone in uniform and all civilians to read the book more than once. You will hear the bursting of shells and the stutter of machine guns ; see the smoke and dust of combat and smell the scent of heroic blood shed for the honour of our country.

Well done, Colonel Francis ! I do hope there will be a successor volume to this book chronicling the saga of immortal deeds of the Indian soldier.

Chennai
17th June 2013

General (Retd) S Padmanabhan
PVSM, AVSM, VSM
Former Chief of Army Staff, Indian Army

PREFACE

History of warfare forms a major part of the history of a nation. The Indian Army was born on 15 August 1947. Our nation builders had given higher priority to peace and progress of the newly born nation, whereas our potential adversaries had expanded their armed forces much beyond their defensive requirements. We were conservative on this aspect.

Accession of Jammu and Kashmir (J&K) with the Union of India was complete on 26 October 1947. The next day, Indian Army was airlifted to Srinagar to save J&K from the Pakistani Raiders comprising of their irregular forces and the tribals of North Western province duly supported by their Army. By the time the leading elements of Indian Army landed at the Srinagar Airfield on 27 October, nearly one third of J&K had been lost to Pakistan.

The delay imposed on the Raiders by Brigadier Rajinder Singh of J&K State Forces and his men between Uri and Baramula and a trick played by a young boy at Baramula, prevented the infiltrators from reaching Srinagar as per their planned time schedule. Added to that was the greed of the Raiders which further delayed them in arsen and looting at Baramula. The bold action undertaken by the first Indian Army Unit that had landed at the Srinagar Airfield on 27 October 1947 prevented the Raiders from having a cakewalk towards Srinagar.

This helped in the landing of more Army units by air. The tenacious holding up of Pak infiltrators at Badgam by a company of brave men contributed to a five hours delay and ultimately denied the contact to the Infiltrators with the Airfield, which was the center of gravity of this battle. Srinagar was finally saved after a pitch battle at the outskirts of the City. Once this was achieved, the Indian Army could divert its attention to other sectors such as Poonch, Naushera and Ladakh. It took more than one year before the vital areas of the J&K State could be secured, though not fully. For a newly born Indian Army, it was a long war.

A few young men had achieved such results, which were considered as impossible until then. To name a few; until 1948 no one is known to have crossed Zojila in winter. Though he took a long time to travel and cross Zojila, which was covered with eight feet of snow; a young captain with his platoon achieved this feat and reached Leh in March 1948. Another landmark achievement was taking the tanks to Zojila with the help the Army Engineers and capturing the Pass with the tanks assaulting the enemy entrenched there.

The cause of 1962 Chinese Aggression was one of territorial dispute. The Indo-Chinese border was (is) not clearly demarcated due to geophysical conditions. Traditional borders were working well during the British Rule in India. Our perception of borderline is different from that of Chinese. Annexation (merger) of Tibet by the Chinese had made things more complicated. Various Treaties signed between the British- India and China were ambiguous. Cartographic maps were nonexistent. There were many lines to indicate the border such as Johnson Line, McCartney MacDonald Line and the McMahan Line. None of them were (are) marked on the ground. Indian Claim Line in NEFA (Arunachal Pradesh) is north of Tawang including Thagla Ridge. The Chinese Claim Line is south of Tawang. The area between the two Claim Lines, mainly Thagla Ridge was the disputed area in NEFA. In Ladakh, Chinese claimed the whole of Aksai Chin and part of Ladakh to be theirs. In nutshell, a complicated territorial dispute existed (and still exists) between India and China since 1947. Political negotiations did not succeed. This set the stage for Chinese Aggression in 1962.

The PLA crossed the traditional border and advanced along three major thrust lines simultaneously during September / October 1962. The western thrust was directed towards Chushul in Ladakh, Thag La Ridge - Namka Chu Tawang - Se La and Bomdi La in the Western Arunachal Pradesh was the Central thrust and towards Walong in the Eastern Arunachal Pradesh close to Indo-Burma (Myanmar) Border was the Eastern Thrust.

Notwithstanding the overall rout the Indian troops suffered in the end, nowhere an Indian soldier was found wanting in terms of dedication or courage while facing the aggressor. When they could not defend the ground, they were asked to deny to the enemy, they fell dying there. Their dead bodies were found either inside their trenches or just outside within their locality.

Chinese aggression on India in 1962 was a major setback to the Nation and compelled India to modernize and enlarge her armed forces. Pakistan would have faced a comparatively weak Indian Armed Forces, had she attempted to annex Kashmir in 1962 along with Chinese Aggression. However, due to fear of international pressure and the poor state of her own armed forces, Pak did not attempt to annex Kashmir then.

By 1965, the Pakistanis saw and assessed that Indian Armed Forces were getting stronger and larger day by day. This they could not tolerate. Therefore, they decided to launch an offensive, with their modernised Army at the earliest with the primary objective of capturing the entire State of J&K. However, as part of their strategic deception they initiated the firefight from down South in the Rann of Kutch in Gujarat. India did not fall prey to the bait and remained balanced to face the major offensive subsequently.

In August 1965, this time better trained and armed, the Pak Raiders crossed the porous border in J&K with a view to foment an uprising against the Govt. They did not succeed. The timely counter measures undertaken by the Indian Army resulted in Pakistan perceiving a threat to their Muzzafrabad. To save themselves of such an embarrassment, Pak Army launched an offensive in Akhnoor area. To counter this threat, Indian Army crossed the border and threatened Lahore. This forced Pakistan Army to pull out from Akhnoor Sector. Similar attempts were also made in Rajasthan Sector. This short war of five weeks ended with Tashkent Agreement. The net result was the creation of Patton Nagar at Village Asal Uttar, the Graveyard of Pakistani Patton Tanks at the scene of the battle and humiliation to the aggressor.

In 1971 due to intense freedom struggle in East Pakistan, very large number of Bengalis from there crossed over the border into India to save themselves from the atrocities committed on them by Pak Army. This created an emergency in the Indian States surrounding East Pakistan. In addition, Pakistan Army carried out raids across the border while the Pak Air Force crossed the air space and engaged in hostile activities. In the West, Pak launched air attacks on many of our airfields located close to the Border.

To overcome this crisis, Indian Army was directed to liberate East Pakistan from Pak Army while containing the Pak Army in the West. Unlike the previous wars, India meticulously prepared for this war. The war started on 3 December 1971. In the East, Indian Army duly supported by the Air Force decided to cross the border from three directions, bypass major oppositions enroute and converge on Dhaka. This was achieved. The war there finally ended on 17 December with the surrender of Pak Army with 91,000 prisoners of war. People of East Pakistan were liberated and Bangla Desh was born.

In the West, Pak's attempt to capture Indian Territory and draw out the Indian resources from the East failed miserably. There were many fierce battles fought at Chhamb, Basantar, Shakargarh, Sialkot and Longewala. In Ladakh, the brave Major Rinchen and his men undertook offensive operations at an altitude beyond 18000 ft and captured more than 800 sq Kms of territory including Turtuk. In all, the Indian Armed Forces came out victorious in 1971.

Since 1971, two military actions of significance took place. Pakistan's attempt to annex Siachen was thwarted just in time in 1984. In 1999, Pakistan's fourth attempt to disrupt the road link between Srinagar and Leh at Kargil was defeated.

This book contains not only stories from wars but also peacetime conflicts since 1947. It provides a synopsis of events, which will help those who would like to comprehend the evolution and growth of the Indian Army and make a mark for themselves in it. This book would have served its purpose if it enables the readers to tell these stories to their children and grand children. It is with great pride, that I dedicate this book as my tribute to those martyrs who sacrificed their life voluntarily under extreme circumstances.

JAI HIND

ACKNOWLEDGEMENT

My desire to write a book of short stories from the History of Indian Army originated during the days of my interactions with Gentlemen Cadets at the Indian Military Academy and officers at various Army schools of instructions, including the Defense Services Staff College, Wellington. I found that a presentation on any subject in the form of a story is always well received and better assimilated by the recipients. I enjoy narrating anecdotes related to the deeds of our Army to many of my civilian friends. Those who heard them were appreciative of these and asked me to put them down in writing for the benefit of others. Some of the serving and retired officers of the Army, Navy and Air Force who heard these stories for the first time, felt that a compendium of these stories would help young aspirants who want to make a career in the Armed Forces. I hereby thank all of them for their encouragement.

I have interacted with many of my former colleagues and friends for the confirmation of the facts of some of the events in which they participated. They were very cooperative and forthcoming with details. I thank all of them too. I believe there are many other stories from the History of Indian Army which have not found its place in this book due to my ignorance. I look forward to receiving suggestions and inputs from the knowledgeable readers so that I can improve this book in the subsequent prints and I thank them all in anticipation. I thank those, who read the draft and had given their views on the subject and the way it has been presented. Their views form part of this book.

My special thanks to the publishers, Vij Books India Pvt Ltd for their guidance and encouragement in converting my work in the book form.

-Author

Short Stories from the Indian Army

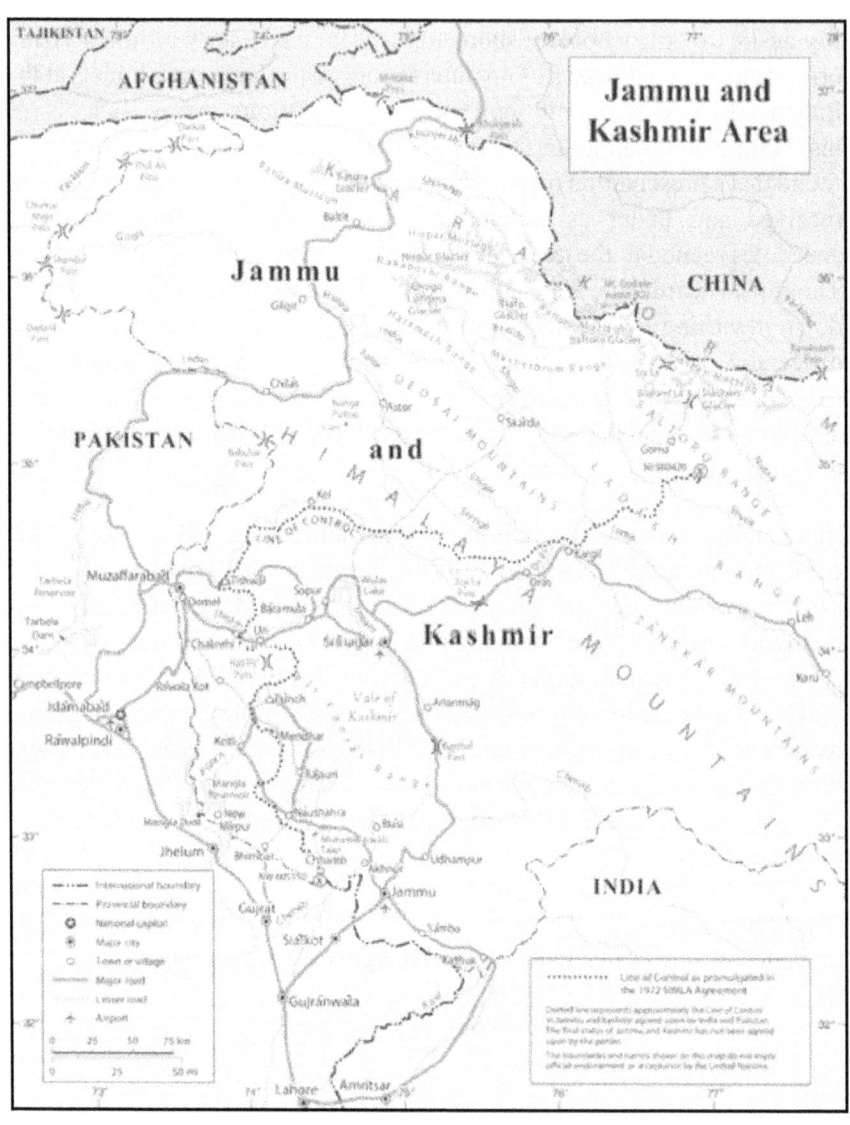

THE FIRST COMMANDING OFFICER

"Two tricks of fortune conspired to cheat the Quaid-l-Azam (Jinnah) of Kashmir Gaddi: the loss of a day and a half in pillaging at Baramula, and reckless bravery of an Indian officer, who with no reserve of men or ammunition made an attack on the invading forces as if he had the whole Army Division at his support"

-A Pakistani Historian

That Indian officer was Lt Col Dewan Ranjit Rai, the first Commanding officer of 1 SIKH who had set the pace for the victory in the first war, which Indian Army had fought after independence.

Lt Col Dewan Ranjit Rai

At the time of India's independence from the British rule, Maharaja Hari Singh ruled the province of J&K, which had neither opted to join with India nor Pakistan. However, Maharaja Hari Singh was suspicious of the intentions of Pakistan; hence, as per the advice of his ministers, he entered into a treaty known as Standstill Agreement with Pakistan. However, Pakistan did not abide by this treaty.

By mid October 1947, the deserters from J&K State Forces, with the active support of Pakistan Army, revolted against the J&K Govt. Pasthun/Mahasud and other tribesmen from the Northwest had joined the revolt and crossed the Pak-Kashmir border on 20 October 1947. Pakistani Raiders had captured the border town of Uri and the hydroelectric power station at Mahur and started to pillage Baramula. Looting of riches from

Baramula town distracted the Raiders from their main objective and delayed their advance towards Srinagar until 26 October.

Some of the eyewitnesses recounted the horrors of murder, rape and looting of the property of the people of J&K. According to Ali Mohamad; a resident of Baramula, "Raiders were murdering young and old, Muslims and non-Muslims, women and children and were taking away truck loads of looted properties including pots and pans and roofing materials and were burning down the houses. They were barbarians; they cannot be born of Muslim parents". Had they not delayed their advance towards their main objective, Srinagar, the entire Valley would have been lost to the Raiders and Srinagar would have become one of the Provinces of Pakistan.

The situation on that day was grim for J&K. The Maharaja had contacted the Prime Minister of India and asked for help. He also agreed to the merger of J&K with the Union of India and accordingly signed the Instrument of Accession on 26 October. The next day the Indian Army landed at Srinagar in J&K.

The acceptance of the accession of J&K with India on 26 October 1947 came with the responsibility of protecting the people and property of J&K, which was under attack by the Pakistani Raiders. Shortage of time and resources and transporting the Army Units over a long distance across difficult terrain in winter added to the enormity of the task for the Indian Army. Terrain in Kashmir Valley was not familiar to Indian Army Units and they needed heavy winter clothing. Severe cold climate had adverse effect on the men, weapon and other materials needed for the operations. The Indian Army did not have the time for a thorough preparation for the impending battles in J&K. It was a firefight; time was at premium; 'fight now or else there will be nothing left to fight for'.

Under these circumstances, 1st Battalion the Sikh Regiment (1 SIKH) which was deployed around Gurgaon in aid to civil authorities for enforcement of law and order and regulating the refugees from Pakistan, was chosen to be inducted by air into the burning Kashmir Valley, to save whatever was possible the very next day. On the same day that the Instrument of Accession was signed, the Commanding Officer (CO) of 1 SIKH, Lt Col Dewan Ranjit Rai was called to the Army Headquarter at New Delhi.

He was given a sketchy briefing and was ordered to take his Battalion from Gurgaon to Srinagar the next morning by hired Dakota aircrafts from civil aviation. A lot about his task was left to his intuition. Clearly, it was a situation wherein, he had to select his task and method of executing it. This was a challenge. But, for the CO of 1 SIKH this was not something out of ordinary. His predecessors were the legends of the Battle of Saragarhi. They always remember the credo, 'difficult will be done and the impossible will be attempted to'.

Major SK Sinha who was dealing with J&K operations at the Army HQs, had briefed the CO and told him that the border town of Uri (63 miles from Srinagar) was in the hands of Raiders and Baramula (35 miles from Srinagar) was being pillaged by them. The unit was required to protect Srinagar city and facilitate the subsequent landings of Indian Army units at the airport.

Early morning on 27 October 1947, 1 SIKH with two-company strength of men and equipment landed in Srinagar Airport, in 30 Dakota aircrafts. It was the first Indian Army Unit to land in Srinagar. Never in the history of warfare was such an airlift undertaken with so little notice and planning. The God was with the Commanding Officer. The landing was perfect.

In the absence of reliable communication or intelligence set up, the CO could not get a clear picture of the enemy activities in the Valley. However he had decided to fight the battle as far away from the airfield as possible with a view to seek the enemy and destroy them in and around Baramula. In spite of the absence of information about the terrain and enemy, the CO boldly decided to take this risk to earn the crucial time for more troops landing at the airfield. (A Pakistani Historian termed this courageous tactical decision as reckless bravery; a compliment!) He knew that fortune favors the bold.

He left behind adequate troops to protect the airfield and moved the rest of his Battalion towards Baramula by early morning 28 October. They came under attack even before the unit could reach Baramula. Therefore, the CO decided to occupy a delaying position, at a dominating high ground in the area of Mile Stone 32 (MS32) between Patan and Baramula with a view to prevent the raiders from advancing towards Srinagar on Baramula Srinagar Road.

Even before the defenses could be prepared fully and coordinated at MS 32 Position, the Raiders attacked it. It was estimated that though they were unorganized; there were over one thousand Raiders moving in small groups from Baramula towards Patan. Sikhs inflicted heavy casualties. The Raiders were seen attempting to surround the Sikhs. To prevent such a grave situation, the CO decided to vacate the MS32 Position and occupy a delaying position at Patan.

The Raiders number increased manifold. Numerically superior Raiders were firing at the Sikhs from close ranges wildly. The CO with his men prevented the Raiders from maintaining contact with the rest of the men and helped them to break contact with the Raiders. With total disregard to their safety, they engaged the Raiders and further delayed the enemy. The battalion was able to occupy the intended delaing position at Patan. However, during this melee, presumably, the Raiders had spotted the CO's Party and brought down heavy volume of fire on them. During this fire fight the CO and a few others were killed. Thus, Lt Col Dewan became the first CO to die in battlefield in the independent India in 1947. For this act of conspicuous bravery in the face of the enemy, exemplary leadership and devotion beyond the call of duty, he was awarded Maha Vir Chakra.

The brave Lt Col Dewan Ranjit Rai, inspired his men to give their best even at the risk of being exposed to enemy fire in the thick of the battle and attained martyrdom. In his glorious death, he achieved many FIRSTS to his credit. The valiant Dewan Ranjit Rai was the first commanding officer to land in Kashmir after J&K joined with India, the first commanding officer to achieve martyrdom in this First Kashmir War and the first commanding officer to be decorated with Maha Vir Chakra. His sacrifice inspired all ranks of the Battalion and they achieved many more glory and honors in this operation to be true to their Regimental motto:

'Nischay Kar Apni Jeet Karun' (With determination, I will be triumphant).

SAVIORS OF THE HEAVEN ON EARTH - GALLANTS GALORE

"Never before .... have so many owed so much to so few"
                                                            -Winston Churchill.

Srinagar Valley is known as Heaven on Earth. No wonder, that Jinnah wanted to annex the entire Kashmir with Pakistan and spend his summer days in Srinagar. However, his desire remained unfulfilled.

After the untimely martyrdom of the CO of 1 SIKH in the battlefield, Major Harwant Singh MC, took over the command of the Battalion. He had six years of service. He was a war experienced brave officer and a popular figure in the Battalion. He fully understood the importance of holding the Raiders far away from Srinagar city and the Airport there and ordered his Battalion to strengthen the delaying position at Patan. From there, besides imposing delay, the Battalion inflicted heavy casualty on the attackers and impeded their movement towards Srinagar.

Having met with stiff resistance, the Raiders changed their method of operation. Instead of attacking the regular Indian Army defenses, they were attempting to bypass them. Hence, Harwant ordered his unit to withdraw towards Srinagar. During the withdrawal, Major Harwant and his brave men fought tough battles and suffered heavy casualty. However, the enemy suffered much more and they were effectively prevented from reaching the airfield and interfering with the landing operations there. By 31 October, the enemy attacks intensified. Their strength increased to about 5,000. They were bypassing the Indian Army delaying positions and heading for Srinagar. In the meantime more Indian troops had landed at the airfield and occupied defenses at Shalteng to prevent the Raiders from entering Srinagar. 1 SIKH and 1KUMAON stood their ground firmly at Shalteng and inflicted heavy causality on the attacking Raiders.

In addition to the Infantry units, tanks of 7 CAVALRY under Lt N G David and the fighter aircrafts of Indian Air Force joined the battle at Shalteng and contributed to the destruction of the Raiders. The attackers were caught between the Infantry firing from the front, the tanks firing from the rear and the aircrafts firing from the top. The tribesmen were routed. The loss was too heavy for them to continue their infiltration operations. Their offensive ended and Srinagar was saved. Thus, the balance tilted in favor of Indian Army. Prime Minister Nehru and Sardar Patel visited Srinagar on 4 November 1947 and addressed the saviors of Srinagar.

From there, 1 SIKH was tasked to relieve Baramula and Uri from the Raiders control. 1 SIKH hunted down and evicted Raiders out of Baramula, liberated the town and got down to relief works. They found that the people of Baramula had suffered beyond description. They provided ration, clothing, shelters and medical aid. There were more than 100 orphaned children in the town. They were sent to the SIKH Regimental Centre Meerut and were rehabilitated.

There is an interesting story of a brave social worker Mahamed Maqbool Sherwani. Sherwani, a resident of Baramula, had suffered the worst atrocities at the hands of the Raiders. He wanted the Raiders to be out of his town. He conceived a novel idea. Sherwani mounted on his bicycle and went around shouting that Indian Army has landed in Srinagar and were advancing towards Baramula.

Raiders believed it and became hesitant to advance towards Srinagar. They further intensified their looting and were busy transporting their loot to Pakistan. This had delayed their advance towards Srinagar. Later, when the raiders realised that young Sherwani had tricked them, they caught hold of him and shot him dead. They also paraded his dead body on a motor cycle, crucified his dead body and saturated it with bullets. However, the crucial delay caused by him with the sacrifice of his life thwarted the goal of the Raiders and saved Srinagar. In honour of Saheed Sherwani as he is known today, who single handed delayed Pakistani offensive for crucial two days; the Army constructed a building at Baramula. It is well maintained and being put to good use for social work.

After Baramula was brought under control, 1 Sikh was ordered to liberate the border town of Uri. This town fell into the hands of Raiders in the beginning of their attack. But they were effectively delayed from moving from Uri towards Baramula by the timely destruction of the only iron bridge on the Uri Nala by Brigadier Rajinder Singh and his men of J&K Army. The brave Brig Rajinder Singh died on 24 October. He was awarded MVC posthumously for his timely action and supreme sacrifice in fighting the Raiders and delaying them.

Brig Rajinder Singh

On 12 December 1947, the enemy ambushed a company of 1SIKH while they were returning to Baramula after liberating Uri. The ambush was broken successfully. The enemy had fled leaving behind more than 300 of their dead. 1 SIKH also had suffered heavy losses; 62 men were killed in the ambush including Jemadar (Naib Subedar) Nand Singh who was a recipient of Victoria Cross in WW II. The brave 29-year old Nand Singh VC was awarded Maha Vir Chakra for his bravery in this action. Thus, he became the highest (VC+MVC) bravery award winner in the Indian Army. Many memorials have been constructed in the Punjab in his honour.

Jamedar Nand Singh, VC

In October 48, 1 SIKH was at Tithwal occupying the front line defenses. Lance Naik Karam Singh commanded one of the forward posts. On the night 13 October 1948, Pakistan attacked this post thrice and suffered heavily. Having failed to capture the post in their fourth attack, the attackers withdrew.

After repulsing four attacks, Karam Singh was left with no ammunition to fight. Knowing additional help was not forthcoming; he shifted from his post to another forward post of his Company, carrying two of his wounded men. Though he himself was wounded, he refused to be evacuated and insisted on fighting the enemy after first aid. His depleted section collected ammunition and occupied another one of the forward most bunkers. The

Lance Naik Karam Singh

attack on his new location was imminent. He deployed his section to bring down maximum fire from the flanks of the attacking enemy.

The enemy launched fresh waves of attacks. He ordered his men to hold the fire until the enemy reached within fifty yards and then they opened fire with full might. The enemy was caught in the deadly enfilade fire from Karam Singh's Section. During the attack, though he was again wounded; he crawled from trench to trench encouraging his men to fight. After repulsing repeated attacks, when he saw two Pakistanis approaching an adjacent bunker, the tenacious Karam Singh came out of his bunker and killed both of them with his bayonet. Thus, the attack was finally repulsed eighth time with heavy loss to the enemy. For this exemplary act of bravery and exceptional courage beyond the call of duty, Karam Singh was awarded Param Vir Chakra. He became an Honorary Captain before he retired. He died on 20 January 1993.

CHM Piru Singh

In the same area, Company Havildar Major Piru Singh of 6 Rajputana Rifles led his Platoon to a ferocious attack to capture an enemy position. The attack was successful but the casualties were heavy. Other than Piru Singh, everyone else from the platoon had either died or was wounded seriously. There was one active enemy bunker still left to be captured. Piru was alone. Yet, unmindful of his loneliness and safety, this brave Rajput advanced toward the enemy charged at the bunker, lobbed a grenade and silenced the last enemy bunker. When the rest of the Company reached their Objective, CHM Piru Singh was found dead due to multiple bullet injury. Those wounded and still alive were evacuated.

For his brave act and exemplary courage, CHM Piru Singh was posthumously decorated with Nation's highest bravery award; PVC. Thus, he had left for the rest of his comrades a unique example of single-handed bravery and determined cold courage. Memorials have been constructed to honour this brave soldier at Junjunu and many other places.

During the First Kashmir War, 1 SIKH won a total of 59 gallantry awards including one Param Vir Chakra, four Maha Vir Chakras (Lt Col Ranjit Rai, Jamedar Nand Singh VC, Naik Chand Singh and Subedar Bishan Singh), 22 Vir Chakras and 32 Mention-in Dispatches in this war. This Battalion was adjudged as the best Infantry Battalion winning maximum gallantry awards while saving the Srinagar Valley from Pakistani raiders.

Lt Gen V R Raghavan, President Center For Security Analysis and former Director General Military Operations, in his book, 'Infantry in India' writes, "1 SIKH with approximately 500 troops, had gained by its fast moves and self reliant actions, two days time against a much larger force of 5,000. This was enough to bring in more troops into Srinagar and the capital was thus saved from falling into enemy hands. The history of Jammu and Kashmir would have been different without this one Infantry Battalion being able to change it decisively."

In this collective saga of courage, it is not easy to single out individuals. Nevertheless, Lt Col Ranjit Rai and Major Harwant Singh will never be forgotten for their inspiring leadership and bold decisions. The decision of the CO to fight away from the airfield and Srinagar city and the delay imposed by Major Harwant Singh and his brave men on the raiders certainly contributed immensely in the saving of the 'Heaven on Earth' from the Raiders. The tanks played a vital role in the overall victory. Lt Col Rajinder Singh the CO, was awarded MVC. (Later Maj Gen MVC Bar)

"O son of Pritha, fortunate are the Kshatriyas when such a righteous battle has, unprovoked, fallen to their lot; they find therein an open door to heaven".

PRATHAM PARAMVIR

"One army man's courage and resilience scripted the history of Jammu and Kashmir"
-Lt Gen (Retd) S K Sinha, Former Governor, J&K

Major Som Nath Sharma

1 SIKH with their bold and swift operations delayed the Raiders and made it possible for other units to land at the airfield without any interference. 4 Kumaon, which was involved in providing aid to civil authorities at the Capital, was airlifted from Delhi to Srinagar to protect Srinagar.

Major Som Nath Sharma was in command of Delta Company, 4 Kumaon. His left hand was in plaster cast due to an injury that he sustained in a hockey match at Delhi a few days earlier. His commanding officer was contemplating to relieve Major Som Nath Sharma from the command of D Company and appoint someone else. Having heard about such a possibility, Major Som Nath Sharma approached his commanding officer and requested that he be allowed to continue as the company commander in spite of his injury. His CO agreed to it.

On reaching Srinagar Airport on 31 October, the Battalion was moved to Badgam to search and destroy a column of raiders, which was hiding around Badgam. However, the patrols sent out could not locate the Raiders. Therefore, the Battalion was ordered to move back to Srinagar main defenses, leaving behind D Company, which was occupying a protective patrol base. At about 1400 hours, a patrol party reported that over 500 Raiders were heading towards D Company. Som Nath quickly readjusted his company to occupy a temporary defense position at a vantage point. This later proved to be a wise decision.

At about 1430 hours on 03 November 1947, the Raiders in large number attacked Delta Company with heavy volume of fire from more than one direction. The Kumaoni's repulsed the attack with heavy casualties on both sides. Another wave of Raiders was seen forming up to launch another attack from a different direction. Major Som Nath, with total disregard to his personal safety readjusted his defenses, moved from trench to trench under heavy fire and encouraged his men to fight. His Company, though outnumbered, had beaten back many attacks and held on to their position for nearly six hours. His last wireless message a few minutes before his death was, "the enemy is only 50 yards from us. We are heavily outnumbered. We are under devastating fire. I shall not withdraw an inch but will fight to the last man and the last round."

During the firefight, Major Sharma saw that one of his light machine guns had only one man crew, hence the firing was slow. The second man of the detachment had been killed. He rushed to that location and with his one hand, he filled the magazines required for the machine gun and helped to continue the fire. While at the light machine gun post, a bomb landed on the ammunition dump next to him and the whole dump exploded. Major Som Nath was killed instantaneously.

On seeing the enemy closing in with the LMG post, Sepoy Dewan Singh stood up with the LMG firing from his hip and killed many of the advancing enemy. His murderous fire had stopped the enemy from further advancing but he fell down dead. His dead body was found riddled with bullets. The rest of the men continued the fight and forced the raiders to withdraw. Indian Air Force Spitfires strafed the fleeing enemy and killed many of them. The Raiders withdrew in utter confusion when their commander was wounded and was being carried on a cot. Thus, the Delta Company eliminated the threat to the Airfield from this direction.

For his valiant act of bravery of the highest order beyond the call of duty and for his supreme sacrifice, the Delta Company Commander, Major Som Nath Sharma was awarded the first Param Vir Chakra in Independent India. Sepoy Dewan Singh was awarded MVC for his exceptional valour in the face of the enemy.

Som Nath Sharma was born on 31 January 1923. His father was a Major General when he retired. Som Nath did his schooling in Sherwood College Nainital and the Prince of Wales Royal Military College, Dehradun. After his training at the Royal Military Academy in 1942, he was commissioned in 8/19 Hyderabad Regiment, which was re-designated as 4 KUMAON in 1947. His uncle was a Captain in that unit. He had served under Colonel K S Thimmaya; who later became the Chief of the Army Staff, in Burma and Malaya during World War II. During this time, his name was 'Mentioned in Dispatch' for saving the life of an injured sepoy by physically carrying him over a distance to a medical aid post.

Before Som Nath left Delhi for Srinagar on 31 October, he told one of his friends that, "Either, I will fight and die in battle and earn Victoria Cross (the highest honor for bravery in British Army) or will one day become the Chief of the Army Staff."

Major Som Nath Sharma fulfilled the first part of his prophecy in his heroic death and won Param Vir Chakra, which is equivalent to Victoria Cross. However, it was his younger brother, General Vishwa Nath Sharma, who became the Chief of Army Staff later in 1988; fulfilling the other part of his elder brother's prophecy. Another brother was Lt Gen Surinder Nath and his sister Kamala was a major in the Army; truly a proud Army family.

No nation was ever built without sacrifice. It is Paramvirs like Major Som Nath Sharma and Mahavirs like Sepoy Dewan Singh, who with their bravery, devotion beyond the call of duty and sacrifices had laid a strong foundation of the Indian Army. They shine as Polestar, guiding the future generations in the profession of safeguarding the integrity of our Nation; Bharath.

SAVIOURS OF NAUSHERA

Pir Panjal Ranges divide Jammu and Kashmir into two halves - the Srinagar Valley to the NE and Punch (Poonch) Valley to its SW. Places like Bhatot, Shopian, Gulmarg and Uri are located at the NE slopes of Pir panjal Ranges. Srinagar, Baramula, Gulmarg, Anantanag, Sopur and Pattan are towns located in the Srinagar valley itself. Whereas, Poonch, Rajauri, Naushera and Riasi (Ma Vaishno Devi Temple) are located SW of Pir Panjal Ranges. Jammu city falls in the area of Shivalik Ranges. Kotli, Mirpur and Alibeg which were part of Kashmir State, are now occupied by Pakistan and known as POK.

Due to its size, good connectivity, scenic beauty and productivity, Srinagar Valley is better-known vis-à-vis the Poonch valley that is relatively smaller in size and where the terrain is mountainous and less productive. The road from Jammu passes through Naushera, Rajauri and on to Poonch. Poonch was connected with Uri and Kotli in the undivided Kashmir through Hajipir Pass. Mirpur was connected to Naushera via Jhangar.

Prior to 1947, the State of Kashmir had its own Army. It was small and spread thin on ground. In 1947, realising that their Maharaja was indecisive, those Kashmiris who wanted Kashmir to join with Pakistan, revolted against the Maharaja. The Pak tribals with the help of Pak Army took control of areas west of line joining Uri - Punch - Naushera and launched attack into Srinagar valley and Poonch Valley.

Pakistani infiltrators crossed the border, entered into J&K on a broad front and headed towards Leh, Srinagar, Poonch and Naushera. They reached the outskirts of Leh, but could not capture it. They captured Uri and Baramula and reached up to Srinagar. Here, they were defeated by the Indian Army and were evicted. However, Poonch was surrounded and the Indian Army could not break the siege until much later. The Pak invaders with tribals had massacred the non-Muslims of Mirpur, Kotli and Jhangar and threatened to capture Naushera. The loss of Naushera to Pakistan would have effectively cut off the entire J&K SW of Pir Panjal Ranges. Therefore, Indian Army units were rushed to defend Naushera and evict the enemy from the Poonch Valley.

Brigadier Mohamed Usman, one of the 16 Brigadiers of the Indian Army at that time, was given the command of 50 PARA Brigade in December 1947 and was tasked to defend Naushera. The challenges were truly formidable to the newly born Indian Army. However, nothing was insurmountable for the young and patriotic Brigadier Usman. The brave men of 1 RAJPUT and 3 RAJPUT Battalions, who were placed under his command, were as loyal and dedicated as their Commander was. For them, glorious death for a cause was more important than life. Besides defending Naushera, Brigadier Usman and the Rajputs vowed to avenge the massacre of nearly 20,000 Hindus and Sikhs at the hands of Pathans and local Muslims at Mirpur and Alibeg in November that year.

Pak employed regular troops along with the militants to attack and capture the areas upto Jhangar by 25 December 1947. They were numerically superior and the proximity to their cantonments was an added asset to them. After the fall of Jhangar, attack on Naushera was building up from Mirpur-Jhangar Axis. In order to save Naushera, this axis of attack and the road for their maintenance had to be denied. Brigadier Usman realized that recapture of Jhangar was essential for the defense of Naushera.

Pickets were established at all tactically important features en-route to Naushera. The units of the Brigade carried out aggressive protective patrolling. The combination of brave Rajputs and Usman was the major cause of worry for the Pakistani leaders who were planning to capture Naushera.

During the first week of February 48, there were numerous patrol clashes around Naushera. Approximately 1,000 Pakistanis surrounded one of the platoon size patrols under Subedar Gopal Singh of 3 Rajput. Undeterred by the numerical superiority, Gopal Singh and his men fought bravely for seven hours and caused heavy causality on the enemy. Sub Gopal Singh led a bayonet charge to break away from the attackers. He was wounded and separated from his platoon. Later Sepoy Sikdar Singh found him and carried him to provide medical aid. Havaldar Mahadeo Singh assumed command and kept fighting until the enemy machine gun fire killed him. For this act of bravery all three; Subedar Gopal Singh, Havaldar Mahadeo Singh and Sepoy Sikdar Singh were honoured with Vir Chakra.

Charlie (C) Company 1 RAJPUT was given the task of guarding the most likely enemy approach to Naushera from the West. The Company commanded by young Lieutenant K S Rathore, was deployed on a low hill known as Taindhar Ridge. 3 Inch Mortars were provided in support of this Company. One of the sections commanded by Naik Jadhunath Singh was guarding the left flank of the Company. C Company was told to hold on to Taindhar Ridge at all cost. Rajputs like Rathore and Jadunath Singh understood the implication of such orders very well.

Naik Jadunath Singh

At the early hours of 6 February, C Company came under enemy attack in waves of hundreds. The enemy strength was estimated to be about 1500; most of them Pathans. The fury of Rajputs defensive fire took a heavy toll on the Pathans. Throughout the engagement, Lt Rathore kept moving from bunker to bunker encouraging his men. Being a Rajput himself, he electrified the men by his presence and they fought tenaciously. At one stage, the enemy closed in within 50 yards of the front line of bunkers. The 3 Inch Mortar detachment commander, Havaldar Dayaram, realizing the gravity of the situation adopted an ingenious method of firing 3 Inch Mortar without secondary charges and dropped the bombs within 50 yards of his position on the attacking enemy with total disregard to the safety of his own life. The attackers suffered heavy casualties and the attack petered out. However, part of the enemy regrouped and attacked on Dayaram's position. Havaldar Dayaram was wounded but the attack was stalled. Thus, the attack on the Company was repulsed with heavy causality on the enemy.

Once again, the attackers attempted to capture Taindhar Ridge; this time from the left flank which was known as Picket 2. Naik Jadunath Singh and his section had prepared additional trenches and were holding the defenses on a broad front. The enemy launched the attack on this section post. At this juncture, Naik Jadunath Singh displayed great valour and superb leadership and moved his men to those additional trenches in such a way that his small force with controlled fire brought down effective fire from whichever direction the enemy assaulted. Frustrated by the murderous fire from Jadunath and his brave men, the enemy retreated in utter confusion. Four of his men were wounded in the first attack. He re-adjusted his section position and was ready for the next attack, which was building up.

The second attack was stronger than the first one. However, the section post did not give in despite it being outnumbered. Most of his men including Jadunath were either wounded or killed. The few still alive were putting up a brave fight. Jadunath took over the Bren gun from the wounded Bren-gunner and resumed firing on the attackers. When the enemy was on the walls of his post, the final volley of fire was so devastating that, what looked like a certain defeat turned into a victory. The attackers stopped short and withdrew, leaving behind more than 300 dead bodies. Thus the post was saved a second time.

The enemy was desperate to establish a foothold on the Taindhar Ridge and relentlessly put in their third attack to capture the Section Post of Jadunath Singh. By then, all men of Jadunath's section were either dead or wounded. Naik Jadunath Singh, himself was wounded second time and was alone. Having left with no other option this brave Rajput came out of the bunker and firing his Sten gun charged on the advancing enemy. The surprised enemy fled in disorder. But this valiant Rajput met a gallant death in his third and last charge when two enemy bullets pierced him in the head and the chest; the last man with last round, had made his ultimate sacrifice; but the Taindhar Ridge was still under the control of Rajputs.

At a most critical stage in the battle for the defense of Taindhar Ridge, C Company held on to their position albeit at a heavy cost. For this act of bravery and supreme sacrifice, Naik Jadunath Singh was decorated with the nation's highest award for gallantry; Param Vir Chakra. His memorial erected at the entrance of Naushera speaks eloquently of his bravery and sacrifice. For his exemplary leadership and act of supreme courage, Lt KS Rathore and Havaldar Dayaram were awarded Maha Vir Chakra.

Once the attack on Taindhar Ridge was blunted, the enemy was held in check. Major General KM Cariappa, (Later COAS and a FM) also from the Rajput Regiment, took over the Command of J&K and ordered the recapture of Poonch and Jhangar. On 18 March 1948 after a fierce battle, the victorious 3 Para Maratha led by Lt Col Virk and 1 RAJPUT entered Jhangar to find a large amount of arms and ammunition and dead bodies of the enemies. Lt Col Virk was awarded MVC for his bravery in this battle.

Thus, the threat to Naushera was eliminated and it was saved from the invaders. Subsequently Poonch was freed and link up took place on 20 November 1948.

LION OF NAUSHERA

Brig M Usman

Brig M Usman was born on 15 July 1912 at Bibipur in Uttar Pradesh in a modest Muslim family. He did his schooling at Varanasi and joined the last Indian batch at Royal Military Academy in Sandhrust in 1932. He was commissioned in Baluch Regiment in 1935. He participated in World War II and saw actions in Burma. By 1947, he rose to the rank of brigadier. At the time of partition, Usman, being a Muslim officer in the Baluch Regiment, was under intense pressure from the Pakistani leaders to opt for the Pakistan Army. However, so strong were the ideals of patriotism and the upbringing by his father that even the ultimate bait of becoming the Pakistan Army Chief proved unsuccessful in convincing Usman. He remained steadfast in his resolve to stay on in the land of his birth and served in the Indian Army. He was transferred to Dogra Regiment from his Baluch Regiment, which went to Pakistan. During the First Kashmir War in December 1947, he was the Commander of 50 (I) Para Brigade that was tasked to defend Naushera.

Defense of Naushera was vital to save the Poonch Valley and Jammu. Pakistani forces attacked and captured areas up to Jhangar with their numerically superior forces by 25 December 1947. It was a major setback for India. Next Pakistani target was Naushera. Brig Usman not only vowed to defend Naushera but also to recapture Jhangar as well. He was so determined to avenge the setback that he promised not to sleep in his bed until he recaptured Jhangar. He used to sleep on the ground with a thin mat.

Major General Cariappa during his visit to the 50 (I) Para Brigade told Brig Usman that the feature, which was dominating Naushera known as Kot, must be secured. Brig Usman launched an operation code named as

'Operation Kipper' and captured Kot and Pathradi successfully. Kot played a significant role in inflicting heavy casualty on the infiltrators when they attacked Naushera with about 10,000 infiltrators a week later. The attack on Naushera was defeated with massive casualty of over 900 dead to enemy. This was one of the fiercest battle in the First Kashmir War and a major turning point in the ongoing war. Brig Usman became a national Hero. The locals called him as Naushera Ka Sher.

He gathered all the orphaned children from the war torn area and created a 'Balak Sena'. They were given proper food, clothing, shelter and education. Some of them were used as messengers during war. They did their job so well that the Prime Minister of India presented three of them with gold watches. Most of them were rehabilitated after the war.

Having stabilized the situation at Naushera he focused his full attention to the recapture of Jhangar which was an important road junction joining the roads from Kotli and Mirpur. He planned this operation meticulously and with his influence, gathered additional resources for the offensive. Before this operation, which was code-named as 'Operation Vijay', he wrote out a letter to all ranks of his Brigade on 15 March 1948. It read as, "Comrades of 50 (I) Para Brigade, Time's come for the capture of Jhangar. It is not an easy task, but I have complete faith in you all to do your best to recapture the lost ground and retrieve the honour of our arms. We must not falter, we must not fail. Forward friends, fearless we go to Jhangar. India expects everyone to do his duty. Jai Hind." Three days later, his troops recaptured Jhangar. Brig Usman asked for his bed and slept on a locally produced Charpoy. Pakistan Govt was so furious that it announced a reward of Rs 50,000 on his head.

He could not bask in the glory of recapturing Jhangar and as the savior of Naushera for a long. He died on 3 July 1948 at the age of 36 years at Jhangar in an artillery shelling. His last words before his death was, "I am dying but let not the territory we were fighting for fall to the enemy". It was a great shock to all those who knew him. The entire country mourned the loss of one of her most beloved sons of India. In a State funeral ceremony which was attended by the then Governor General Lord Louis Mountbatten, Prime Minister of India Pandit Jawaharlal Nehru, Union Minister Maulana Abdul Kalam Azad and Sheikh Abdullah, his body was laid to rest at Jamia Milia University, New Delhi.

He was the senior most Indian Army Officer to die in battle in the First Kashmir War. For his bravery of exceptional order and dedication to his duty, he was decorated with Maha Vir Chakra.

Brig Usman was a simple, compassionate, benevolent and charismatic leader who was deeply religious and fair minded. He remained a bachelor and spent his income for charitable purposes. Most of all he was an inspiring leader. Brig Usman was indeed an epitome of valour, patriotism and nationalism. It is because of him that Naushera is an integral part of India today. His exceptional professional acumen, raw courage, unwavering belief, ingenuity and sense of patriotism will be remembered forever. His steadfast loyalty to the mission and the troops he commanded, exemplary personnel courage and resoluteness against odds will continue to inspire generations of soldiers.

His phenomenal success in the battle of Naushera after capturing Kot and Phirthal and later recapture of Jhangar is a fine manifestation of his inspiring leadership under adverse conditions. Brigadier Mohammed Usman set an example of personal courage, exceptional qualities of leadership and devotion to duty, keeping high the finest traditions of the Indian Army.

His memorials at Naushera and at the campus of Jamia Milia University stand testimony to this true son of India. Bravery was part of his childhood and his death. He was a brave soldier all the way.

THE GATEWAY TO LADAKH

The picturesque town of Skardu is located in the 10 km wide and 40 km long Skardu Valley, at the confluence of the Indus and the Shigar River, at an altitude of nearly 8,200 feet. This was a tehsil headquarter and the winter capital of Ladakh in the olden days; but not anymore; today it is a tourist attracting headquarter town of Skardu District of Gilgit Baltistan Region with regular air service in Pakistan Occupied Northern Areas.

Until August 1947, J&K State comprised of Jammu Region, Kashmir Valley, mountainous Ladakh District and Gilgit Region. (Gilgit was leased to Govt of India (British) and a Governor administered it) The Britishers handed back this region to the Maharaja of J&K just before the partition of India. Hindus predominantly populated Jammu Region, Ladakh by Buddhists, Kashmir Valley and Gilgit Region had Muslim majority. Pakistan expected that Maharaja of J&K would opt to join with Pakistan. However, it did not happen.

By 25 October 1947, the raiders from Pakistan had captured nearly half of Kashmir Valley and were poised to enter Srinagar. Having realized that his remaining State Forces were incapable of defending the State from the large-scale offensive by the raiders, the Maharaja decided to join with India and signed the Instrument of Accession. Until then Indian Forces could not and did not enter into the State of J&K.

Along with the fragmented and tormented State of J&K, came their armed forces comprising of eight Infantry battalions, four Brigade Headquarters and one battery of artillery guns. They were spread all over the State. Their fighting potential had reduced considerably due to large-scale desertion of Muslim Troops. Within the constraints of resources available, priority was give to stabilize the situation in the Kashmir Valley and Naushera before the higher mountainous region could be dealt with; for in the Northern region, even Pakistanis could not have made progress in their operations due to heavy snow during winter.

Ladakh had not seen a wheeled vehicle until 1948. There were no roads capable of taking mechanical transport. Ladakhis used mules, yak and donkeys for load carrying. There was a track between Gilgit and Leh that

Zojila

passed through Skardu. This was the main approach to Ladakh before 1947. Leh could also be approached from Gilgit via Nubra Valley from the Northern side.

The present road alignment between Kargil and Srinagar was the least preferred track as Zoji La was difficult to cross. Another track existed from the South between Leh and Manali in Himachal Pradesh. The major traffic to Ladakh from Kashmir Valley was only through Gilgit Region. (The motorable road from Srinagar to Leh via Sonamarg, Zoji La, Dras, and Kargil was constructed in 1955 by the Army Engineers.)

On 01 November 1947, Gilgit was taken over by the Muslim elements of J&K State Forces with the help of Pak Army after the Governor, Brigadier Ghansar Singh was arrested. Thus, the Gilgit Region was lost. Due to severe winter, and lack or resources, further military operation was not undertaken. Pakistani forces consolidated their gains and were preparing for the offensive in the following summer months.

After the loss of Gilgit to Pakistan, it was appreciated that the next move of Pak Forces will be to advance towards Balistan, capture Leh, and control the entire Ladakh region. Skardu was the Gateway to Ladakh. Without the capture of Skardu, no meaningful military operation could have been undertaken towards Ladakh.

With the view to prevent the Pakistani invaders from using Skardu Axis, it was decided to occupy Skardu with the available J&K State Forces.

Accordingly a Company of 6 J&K Infantry Battalion which was then located at Leh, was sent to defend Skardu and deny the use of this approach to Pakistani Forces from Gilgit to Leh. About a platoon worth of State forces was left behind to defend Leh.

In spite of heavy snowfall, the Company of 6 J&K Infantry under the Command of Major Sher Jung Thapa reached Skardu by the first week of December 1948. The defense of Skardu was based on Kharphocho Fort, which was located on a slope overlooking Skardu (40 feet above the town). The troops were inadequate to defend Skardu. The Muslim troops in the Company were looking for an opportunity to desert and join Pak Forces. Two of the Muslim signalers had already deserted. That left with no one else other than Maj Thapa who knew how to operate the wireless telegraphy sets.

Kharphocho Fort at Skardu

Thapa was a tenacious officer. He very well understood the importance of holding Skardu at all cost. He organized his defenses and stocked his position for a prolonged fight. Later, some additional troops were given to him, but it was never adequate. Pakistan launched 'Operation Sledge' with the aim of capturing Ladakh. Approximately two-battalion worth of regular and local militia forces commenced their advance in the first week of February 1948 from Gilgit. Skardu was attacked with 600 strong force on 11 February. In spite of numerical superiority, Pak forces failed to penetrate the defenses. They massacred a large number of Hindus and Sikh civilians who were outside the fort.

Having failed in their attempt to capture, they invested the Fort with about 200 men and with the rest, they advanced further towards Zoji La after crossing the high Himalayan ranges with a view to bypass Skardu and approach Leh via Kargil. Small party of raiders also attempted to reach Leh via Nubra Valley. A brave 17-year-old (Young) Rinchen and his band of patriotic volunteers thwarted this attempt.

In the mean time, attempts were made to reinforce Skardu unsuccessfully. The enemy had asked for surrender, which Thapa refused. He was given an option to withdraw but he did not withdraw. Attempts were also made to reinforce Leh. In this effort, Capt Prithvi Chand of 2 DOGRA with 40 of his men achieved a humanly impossible task of crossing Zoji La during winter for the first time and succeeded in reaching Leh on 13 March 1948.

By May 1948, the Gilgit Forces gained control over Zoji La, Dras and Kargil and were advancing towards Leh. It was a small force without adequate logistic support. With this threat, the importance of denying Skardu Axis to enemy became even more crucial to prevent any build up for the attack on Leh.

To reinforce Leh by air, the locals constructed a temporary airstrip on the banks of Indus River. The first Dakota aircraft landed successfully on 24 May 1948. Air Commodore Mehar Singh DSO and Major General Thimayya were on board with some troops. Thus, the first wheeled transport that some of the Ladakhis saw was an aircraft. From then on, Leh was reinforced with men and materials by air throughout the summer months.

Skardu still holding out, threat to Leh now was from Kargil. However, Pak forces could not build up further, without the Gilgit Skardu axis being available to them. The tenacious Thapa would not budge. Skardu was intact still under his command. On 13 August 1948, after six months of siege, Gilgit Forces reinforced with Pak regulars and Chitral Forces launched a massive multi-directional attack on the defenses of Skardu and captured it. All officers and men were taken as POW and later killed except Lt Col Sher Jung Thapa.

Having lost the gateway to Ladakh, Zojila had to be cleared urgently. 77 Brigade was tasked to recapture Zojila and clear the enemy now threatening Leh. 77 Brigade from Srinagar advanced upto Zoji La and had fought some of the toughest battles in the high altitude with 15 Punjab (Patiala) and 2/8 GR achieving feat beyond imagination.15 Punjab was awarded seven MVCs, 17 VrCs and the Battle Honour of Zojila. 2/8 GR marched on foot all the way from Manali to reinforce Leh in time. To complete the operations before the onset of winter, Maj Gen Thimmaya decided to use the tanks for the capture of Zojila.

On 01 November 1948, 7 CAVALRY achieved a feat, which no other army anywhere in the world had achieved before. They took their tanks to a height of 3500 m in dismantled state and reassembled them there. The assault by the tanks shocked Pakistanis and drove them away. Two companies of MADRAS SAPPERS were instrumental in achieving this feat.

By the end of November they evicted the raiders from Zojila, Dras and Kargil and linked up with Leh. Thus Ladakh was saved.

The situation in the valley was tilting in favour of Indian Army. Pakistani raiders were forced to beat a hasty retreat and withdrew to Skardu.

The siege of Skardu; the Gateway to Ladakh, lasted over six months.
Had it not, Ladakh would have been annexed with Gilgit by the Pakistanis forever.

Dakota aircrafts landed in a temporary airfield under adverse conditions at Leh.
Had it not, Ladakh would have been annexed with Gilgit by the Pakistanis forever.

The tanks were taken to Zoji La by 7 CAV with the help of MADRAS SAPPERS.
Had it not, Ladakh would have been annexed with Gilgit by the Pakistanis forever.

Many brave heroes like Thapa, Prithvi Chand and Rinchen had achieved impossible feats.
Had it not, Ladakh would have been annexed with Gilgit by the Pakistanis forever.

By the end of 1948, the raiders were also evicted from the Srinagar Valley and Poonch was liberated. However, some territory captured before 26 October 1947 and the Gilgit Region remained under Pak control. Having realized the resources constrains to recapture the Gilgit Northern Areas and having placed the trust in UNO's mediation, a ceasefire agreement was signed and the existing line of troop holding, known as 'Cease Fire Line', became a temporary border between India and Pakistan on 01 January 1949. (This CFL, with minor changes, was later converted into Line Of Control (LOC) on 03 July 1973 post 1971 war with Pakistan)

Thus, the erstwhile Kingdom of J&K was divided, with approximately 101,000 sq km area remaining with India and 86,000 sq km with Pakistan. Though Ladakh was saved, Skardu remained with Pakistan.

THAPA THE TENACIOUS

In 1947, while Pakistan wanted to annex Kashmir Valley for obvious reasons, it was the greed for the riches of the Buddhist Monasteries in Ladakh that lured them to this land of Lamas. For the newly born India and Indian Army, defense of Ladakh was far more challenging than the rest of the J&K due to the nature of its terrain and lack of means of communication.

If one has to attribute the successful defense of Ladakh against Pakistani offensive in 1947- 48, the name that comes on the top of the list is that of Sher Jung Thapa. His tenacity and perseverance against heavy odds is most commendable. It is likes of Thapa who achieve results beyond expectations.

Thapa was born in a traditional military family at Abbotabad in June 1908. His father and grandfather were distinguished soldiers. Later his father shifted his family to Dharamsala where Thapa completed his college education. Thapa was an excellent hockey player. He played for their college team that used to participate in local tournaments.

1 Gorkha Regiment had their training center at Dharamsala. Captain Douglas Gracy was their Adjutant. Capt Gracy who was a member of the 1 Gorkhas hockey team was highly impressed by Thapa's sportsman sprit and took upon himself to shape the future of young Thapa. With his guidance and help, Thapa was commissioned as an officer in the J&K State Forces in 1932. The relationship born at the hockey fields of Dharmsala between Gracy and Thapa had an unimaginable consequence in due course of time.

J&K State had a small Army. The 5th and 6th Battalions of J&K Infantry were deployed in Gilgit and Ladakh in 1947. Unfortunately, the 5th Battalion which was deployed at Gilgit switched their loyalty and went over to Pakistan. The 6th Battalion was located at Leh where Thapa was commanding a Company with the rank of Major.

By December 1947, having lost Gilgit region to Pakistan, it was decided to prevent Pakistanis from advancing further into Ladakh by denying the major axis, Gilgit Leh, at Skardu. Accordingly, Thapa was given the command of two companies of 6 J&K Battalion and was promoted to the rank of Lt Col. Thapa left Leh on 23 November 1947 and reached Skardu on 3 December, walking through the heavy snowfall.

He had initially two officers and 75 men. In spite of adverse terrain and climatic conditions, Skardu was later reinforced with additional troops. By February 1948, Skardu defenses had about 130 men that was far less to defend Skardu against the onslaught of over 600 Pakistani attackers. There was only one wireless set for rearward communication. Communication within the company was only through the runners.

Thapa was tasked to deny Skardu until the defense of Leh was organized. He studied the overall situation and realised that he had a long and hard fight ahead of him. He deployed his meager resources most economically and decided to fight the enemy even before they reached Skardu. Accordingly, he had established two early warning and delaying positions of platoon strength each on either side of River Indus, about 32 kilometers from main defenses and the rest were deployed at Skardu Fort providing protection to the locals.

On the night of 9/10 February 1948, Pakistanis attacked the platoon on the left bank of the Indus River. Captain Krishna Singh, their commander, was murdered in cold blood and the few survivors were led off to Gilgit. The platoon on the Right Bank of the river, commanded by Captain Nek Alam of Muslim troops, simply raised their hands and surrendered to the enemy. The raiders then proceeded to Skardu. They passed through many small villages but not a whiff reached Skardu of their impending arrival.

On 11 February, the tribals attacked Skardu. They were met with a controlled hail of accurate fire from the defenders. The attack was defeated. The tribals now poured their wrath on the town below. It was pillaged and then they retreated in total disorder, leaving behind their ten dead men and one wounded. They also left behind a medium machine gun and a 2-inch mortar. During the mayhem, they killed a large number of civilians including Sri Amar Nath, the District Officer. The defenders had seven Other Ranks killed and one Officer and 15 Other Ranks wounded.

On 13 February 1948, Skardu was reinforced with one more officer and 70 men. Thapa had reorganized his defenses with early warning elements deployed in all likely approaches. Between 15 February and 16 March, a number of clashes took place and in all cases, the defenders came away the better. Thapa was on the move from one post to another whenever the enemy tried to ingress into the defenses. His presence and his bold action encouraged his men. The fighting raged on until 4 April. Captain Ajit Singh; one of his Company Commanders was wounded severely but did not leave his post. They could not collect drinking water for days. Men lived with just two chapattis and a piece of dry apple or apricot per meal.

Having unsuccessfully attempted to reinforce Skardu, Thapa was given the option of withdrawing from Skardu. Had he done so the consequences would have been disastrous. The Kashmir Valley was still in turmoil. Leh was not yet adequately reinforced. He realized that the longer he holds Skardu the greater will be the chances of saving Ladakh. Most of all he was concerned with the safety of the civil population living at Skardu. They would certainly be murdered if they fall in the hands of the Pakistani tribals. Hence, the tenacious Thapa decided to stay on and fight to finish.

Frustrated with many unsuccessful attempts to capture Skardu and having suffered a heavy loss, the Pakistanis decided to siege Skardu. It was isolated from all sides. On 17 June, the raiders sent a messenger under a flag of truce. He carried a letter demanding the surrender of the garrison from the Pakistani Colonel addressed to Lt Col Thapa. The messenger was sent away with a refusal.

July; a month that would herald summer and ripening of fruit, brought only continued misery to the defenders. Barley that was grown within the garrison was now the main diet. Malnutrition had set in. The physique of the defenders now displayed clothes hanging on shrunken frames. By August, the garrison was reduced to two 'chappatis' of barley and a cup of tea per day.

12 August witnessed yet another determined attack by 200 raiders. Hand to hand combat ensued. With ammunition running low, the last box of ammunition from the Fort was used. The attack was repulsed; the raiders withdrew leaving behind a pile of their dead. This was the swansong of the garrison; they had carried the day yet again. It was however the beginning of the end. What ammunition remained were 10 cartridges with each rifleman. That was all, no grenades, no bombs, nothing.

The garrison on 14 August 1948 consisted of Lt Col Thapa, four Officers, one JCO and 35 Other Ranks; apart from the civilians. By then, the overall situation in J&K and Ladakh had improved considerably. The relative importance of Skardu had diminished with the reinforcement received at Leh by air.

Thapa had left with no other option but to leave the Fort or starve to death. When the raiders took charge of the Fort after six months and three days of siege, the Muslim's were led away, the remaining were murdered. Captain

Ganga Singh, the Adjutant was tied to the ground and shot. The fate of the civilians and womenfolk is best left to the imagination. It was a repeat of the events at Baramula. Lt Col Thapa and his Sikh orderly, Sepoy Kalyan Singh were not harmed. Only Pakistanis knew the reason for this.

General Sir Douglas Gracey, KCB, KCIE, CBE, MC was the Commander-in-Chief of the Pakistan Army in February 1948. From his office at Rawalpindi, he had full survey of the war of Jammu and Kashmir. The war in Gilgit/Balistan region of the Himalaya's held a certain interest for him at a personal level. He had been apprised of the happenings and in particular, the defiant stand being taken by the garrison of Skardu. He was also informed that a Lieutenant Colonel Sher Jung Thapa commanded this garrison.

Today, it would be a matter of conjecture what thoughts must have crossed the mind of General Gracey on learning about the garrison commander of invincible Skardu. Doubtlessly his reflections would have taken him back a quarter of a century to 1924 when he was the Adjutant of the 1 Gorkha Regimental Centre and he had played hockey against a young lad at Dharamshala whom he had encouraged to work hard and seek a future in the armed forces. Lt Col Thapa was that young man he had befriended. He must have been proud of his progeny.

When the fall of Skardu was imminent, strict orders would emanate, that Lt Col Thapa is to be extended all courtesies of war and his person is not to be harmed. No one dared disobey an order from the Commander-in-Chief. Fate thus intervened and gave to Lieutenant Colonel Thapa a reprieve from what would have been certain death at the hands of the raiders.

What will live on forever, is the heroic stand at Skardu that was possible because of one man alone; Lieutenant Colonel Sher Jung Thapa. Whether it was in siting his weapons, fortifying his bunkers and defenses and most importantly, rallying his command to surmount every conceivable hardship; that his majestic personality shone like a radiant star. True to his name, he was the LION in the BATTLE. The siege of Skardu will always be linked to Lieutenant Colonel Thapa and his sheer will to go on despite all odds.

The cease fire between India and Pakistan came into effect on 1 January 1949. A few weeks later, Lieutenant Colonel Thapa returned from Pakistan to a very warm welcome. He was awarded the Maha Vir Chakra and was promoted to be Brigadier.

Brig S J Thapa

Soon after ceasefire, Prime Minister Jawaharlal Nehru visited Kashmir Valley and addressed the troops. General Thimayya, Commander of 19 Infantry Division, also addressed the officers. In his address, General Thimayya said; "*My strategy to save Ladakh was to hold on to Skardu at all costs so that Pakistani forces may be prevented from reaching Kargil and Leh. Fortunately, I had the right man in Skardu to fulfill this mission. No words can describe the gallantry and leadership of Lieutenant Colonel Sher Jung Thapa who held on to Skardu with hardly 250 men for six long months. It is one of the longest sieges in the annals of war. While ordering him to defend Skardu to the last man and last round, I had promised to send him reinforcements and supplies. Unfortunately, neither could reach Skardu. I also tried to airdrop more rations and ammunition but these were merely helping the enemy. At the end of six months, when he completely ran out of ration and ammunition, I asked him to surrender. My General Staff Officer, Colonel Shri Ram Oberoi, gave this order to the gallant officer on radio in August 1948. Thapa's response is etched on my mind and I can never forget it. He said, 'I know that I cannot hold out without rations and ammunitions. General Thimayya has failed me. I know the fate my troops will meet after surrendering to the enemy. I cannot do anything now against the enemy but I will certainly take revenge in my next life.'"*

Officers of this stamp make great armies and great nations.

THE TEENAGE HERO

"Our intelligence revealed that our repeated attacks in Nubra Valley were foiled by the personal valour of a 17 year old boy named Chhewang Rinchen; had we succeeded at Skuru, there would then have been no real obstacle to our capturing Leh."

-Col Mohammad Yusuf, Pakistan Army

Chhewang Rinchen was seventeen years old when decorated with his first of many gallantry awards for bravery in battle; a Maha Vir Chakra (MVC). I do not know of any other hero who was decorated with MVC at such a young age in the Indian Army or received so many awards for bravery in war.

In 1947, the local militia and Pakistani Forces captured Gilgit in an uprising. Further advance to capture Ladakh from Gilgit through the direct and relatively easier approach via Skardu was denied by the Tenacious Thapa (Brig Sher Jung Thapa MVC). Zoji La was blocked with heavy snow. The third approach, which is longer and treacherous from Gilgit to Leh via Nubra valley, was along Shyok River, which runs parallel to and North East of Indus River. A small force could advance through this route and threaten Leh via Nubra Valley and Khardung La (highest pass).

Young Rinchen Chewang was a true son of the soil. He was born in 1931 in the village of Sumur in Nubra Valley. One of his ancestors was conferred with the title of Lion of Ladakh for his bravery. Rinchen's mother was known as the Mother of Nubra Valley for her compassion. In Ladakhi, Chhewang means hero and Rinchen means full of life. Rinchen was true to the literal meaning of his name. He received his primary education from Mr. Stanzin, a Ladakhi Christian missionary. For secondary education, Rinchen was sent to Leh.

In 1947, disappointed with the Treaty of Accession, Pakistan attacked across the borders of J&K including Gilgit and Balisthan. While the raiders annexed a large chunk of J&K and Gilgit Region, Ladakh remained relatively safe due inadequate road communication. Zoji La (the pass that connects Leh with Srinagar Valley) was blocked due to heavy snow. Skardu was holding out against Pakistani attack and it was under seize. Therefore, the raiders could not make further progress along this approach. Under these circumstances, Pakistani raiders had decided to advance towards Leh along the third approach through Nubra astride the River Shyok and capture Leh. There was nothing Ladakhis could do to thwart this attempt. Loss of Ladakh was in the horizon.

Even after realizing the gravity of the threat, a sense of helplessness prevailed in the minds of civil govt officials and military leaders of India. Indian resources were fully stretched. Naturally, Ladakhis were unhappy. However, they did not sit back for the catastrophy to descend on them. They dread living in Pakistan. Under these uncertain circumstances, a bright spark appeared in the form of Captain Prithvi Chand. This young Budhist Officer from Lahaul volunteered against all the sane advises of his superiors and friends and undertook a hazardous journey to cross Zoji La on foot during the peak winter season along with a platoon of his men and mules. Unbelievable happened. He and his men reached Leh and a ray of hope was now visible. He got involved in enrolling volunteers to fight along with his Platoon against Pak raiders in Nubra Valley. He called them National Guards.

Rinchen was though young, he was very perceptive and patriot. He did not like to lead his future life in Pakistan ruled Ladakh. For him the comfort of his religion and safety of his mother land was more important than his studies. And he left his schooling and volunteered to join the National Guards when he was a boy of 17 years.

After a period of ten days training, he was sent with Subedar Bhim Chand to raise a local unit in the Nubra Valley. Within a period of one month, a company of Nubra Guards was raised and trained. They were immediately deployed in the Nubra Valley against Pakistani raiders along the Northern banks of Shyok River.

Rinchen's first victory as commander of 28 strong Nubra Guards came at La Chhuruk, which was a picket, held by Pakistanis. It took a few days to cross the rivers and scale different peaks to reach the enemy picket at La Chhuruk from the least expected direction. Nubra Guard party surprised the Pakistanis and killed all enemy soldiers holed up in the picket. The Post was captured along with arms and ammunition left behind by the enemy. The thrill of his first victory was enhanced by the capture of arms, ammunition and ration which was a rare commodity in the remote areas and a great morale-boosting factor for the Nubra Guards.

Pakistanis posed yet another threat to Leh from Kargil. This had to be tackled immediately. Therefore, leaving behind Rinchen and 23 of his men, the rest were withdrawn from Nubra Valley. Rinchen and his men heroically defended the Shyok and Nubra valleys using tactics like shooting from different spots or lighting fires on many peaks to trick the enemy into believing that Indian troops were encircling them. The Pakistanis were unaware of the reduction of forces from Nubra for nearly a month.

Rinchen used his influence with Ladakhi leaders, managed to get more weapons and enrolled many more locals to strengthen the defense of Nubra Valley. Pakistani forces when realized that Nubra Valley was being guarded only by the local Guards, planned to resume their advance towards Khardung La through Nubra Valley. Preparation to cross Shyok River was observed by the local Ladakhis.

Having found out the details of the enemy crossing place across Shyok River, Rinchen and his men were waiting in an ambush for the enemy to cross the River. The next day, about 10 in the morning, the Pakistani troops got into the boat and were crossing the the River. When the boat was in the middle of the River, heavy volume of accurate fire was brought down on them by Rinchen and his men. All of them were either killed or drowned. The enemy on the other side of the River left their arms and ammunition and ran away. Thereafter they never tried to cross the Shyok River.

Rinchen's valuable contribution to the security of Ladakh was recognized and he was promoted to the rank of Jemadar (Naib Subedar) at the tender age of 17 years. By August 1948, the enemy had attempted many a times to capture dominating places in the Nubra Valley but all in vain. Jemadar Chhewang Rinchen and his Guards immobilized the enemy for nearly two months.

In September, he was tasked to capture the enemy company headquarter position, at a place known as Lama House. This was an extremely difficult task and entailed four days of marching through treacherous country, including crossing a mountain feature over 17000 feet high. He succeeded in capturing the objective with heavy casualties to the enemy and they captured 13 rifles and one Sten gun. Rinchen's force eliminated the major portion of the enemy platoon and the rest ran away in their under-clothes. Among the dead was their platoon commander, Sergeant Major Mota Hassan of Gilgit Scouts. Rinchen had killed him in hand to hand fighting with a bayonet and captured his sten gun. This sten gun was later presented to the Hall of Fame at Leh and lies there.

Again, on 22 December 1948, he was detailed to attack the enemy's last position in Leh Tehsil area. It took him six days to reach his objective. He had to go over high mountain features above 21000 ft. Though his platoon suffered from frostbite heavily, he kept his men going through his outstanding and exemplary leadership. He attacked two enemy posts and captured them.

On 01 January 1949, a ceasefire was declared by both countries and the existing frontline of the troops on both sides had become the Cease Fire line (CFL).

For his contribution to the war efforts of saving Ladakh during 1948, outstanding leadership and personal act of bravery in the face of the enemy, Jemadar Rinchen Chewang was awarded Maha Vir Chakra.

Jemadar Rinchen had also received many tributes from military leaders. Lt Gen ML Chibber (Retd) wrote, *"I noticed the uncanny mountain sense he displayed while moving for an attack on an enemy picket. He had God given instinct to choose the most appropriate, even the most hazardous route, to surprise the very vigilant enemy. I realised his being a man who comes into his own in battles"*. Colonel Prithvi Chand, himself a winner of many laurels and the mentor of Rinchen said, *"Rinchen turned out to be an inspiring leader. He was a fearless man and highly patriotic. He volunteered to take part in several battles and raids and succeeded in all of them against heavy odds."*

Many more glories were in the offing to this great soldier. Jemadar Rinchen MVC was the first 17-year old to be awarded with MVC for bravery in battlefield; this would earn a permanent career in the Indian Army. A commission in the Indian Army as an officer was the most sought after way of leading the rest of his life for this brave, young and highly decorated warrior. He and the men of Nubra Guards, which formed part of the National Guards, had saved their Nubra Valley. In turn, this saved Ladakh from falling into the hands of Pakistani raiders in 1948. The youngest Jemadar Rinchen was also the youngest winner of MVC in the Indian Army. He lived to become a legend of many battles and heroic deeds; some of them beyond human endurance. He had also achieved many FIRSTS including the Honorary Colonel of The Ladakh Scout. (In 1952 the National Guards was converted into J&K Militia. By 1961 Rinchen was promoted to the rank of Major and was serving with 7 J&K Militia. Later on in 1963, J&K Militia was re-designated as LADAKH SCOUTS.)

The First Kashmir war ended with the UN intervention on 31 December 1948. Three fifth of the J&K was with India and the rest two fifth were retained by Pakistan. UN mandated that the Pakistani Forces be vacated from J&K. India was allowed to retain some forces for the maintenance of law and order there. Upon the withdrawal of Pak forces from J&K, a plebiscite was to be held to decide the future of J&K. However, this never happened. Pakistan once again attempted to annex Kashmir in 1965 but failed to achieve any success.

PRELUDE TO 1962 WAR

"A great soul-awakening such as it, has never had in all its history."
-Former President Dr Sarvepalli Radhakrishnan

The Indo Chinese border settlement talks did not produce any tangible results in the forties and fifties. The Chinese persisted and remained adamant with their claim of 13000 sq kms of Indian Territory along the northern border. Several border incidents took place between 1954 and 1959. In the early sixties, reports were received that the People's Liberation Army (PLA) was building roads close to the Indian Territory. With the deteriorating relationship with China, it became essential to have a permanent presence of security forces close to the border at the Tri-junction of India/China/Pakistan near the base of Karakoram Pass. Daulat Beg Oldi village (DBO), located just 8 kms from the Border with China, at an altitude of 16,200 ft was selected off the map as a suitable location for one of the many such all weather military posts. This flat piece of ground was also found potentially suitable for a temporary airfield for small aircrafts. Some one had to physically ascertain the suitability.

Major Rinchen Cheewang MVC, of J&K Militia, was chosen for this demanding task of confirming the suitability of DBO for establishing a border post there. It entailed a trek through 120 km of the most inhospitable terrain on the planet earth in freezing temperature and deadly snow blizzards. Rinchen, a man of many FIRSTS, enjoyed this kind of challenge and adventure. He and his chosen men who were born and grew up in these mountains were not called for nothing as Ibex. They loved their mountains and the challenges it posed. For them the high altitude rugged mountains were their backyard play field.

In August 1961, Rinchen and his men set off on their trek towards DBO. Winter was approaching and the weather was deteriorating fast. The march proved to be extremely difficult. When the party reached Saser La; a pass near DBO, they were forced to take rest at the base for two days before crossing the Saser La.

On September 3, 1961, the party reached the Chip Chap river after crossing the infamous 'Gateway to hell'; not far from DBO. The next morning, when he woke up, Rinchen noticed the hoof marks of camels and horses as well as tread marks left by heavy vehicles. He began to suspect that the Chinese were already occupying the Indian Territory. After crawling through difficult terrain and a high pass, he reached a water point. He climbed a small plateau, and with the help of his binoculars saw that the Chinese were housed in a double-storied building. A large number of Chinese soldiers were seen engaged in road and house building activities. Three vehicles were parked close by. Rinchen immediately informed of this to his Headquarters, which was relayed to Delhi.

Gen J N Chaudhry presenting Sena Medal

The presence of Chinese was later confirmed by two surveillance planes, which took pictures. Based on the findings and recommendations of Rinchen, it was decided to establish a permanent military Post at DBO. Once again, Major Rinchen was tasked to lead his Battalion to DBO. This time another route was selected. According to the estimates, this should have taken 15 days for the unit to reach DBO. Whereas, Rinchen lead them and reached DBO in just five days and the post was established before the Chinese crossed the border in 1962. The timely establishment of a military post saved DBO from falling into the hands of Chinese. There is a functional airfield at DBO. This is the highest in the world.

For this act of exemplary service, indomitable courage and leadership, Major Rinchen MVC, was awarded Sena Medal.

WINNER IN THE BATTLE OF CHUSHUL

*"How can a Man Die Better than Facing Fearful Odds,
For the Ashes of His Fathers and the Temples of His Gods?"*

- At the Chushul War Memorial

A battle is won or lost by troops, whereas, a war is won or lost by political leaders and generals. In 1962 Chinese captured a vast Indian Territory in the North-East Frontier Agency (NEFA) now known as Arunachal Pradesh and Ladakh and won the war. Notwithstanding the outcome of the war, there were battles in which individual soldiers, sub units and units of the Indian Army had demonstrated remarkable resilience under the most unfavorable conditions and prevented the enemy from winning in those battles. One such battle was fought for the defense of Chushul, strategically an important communication center in Ladakh.

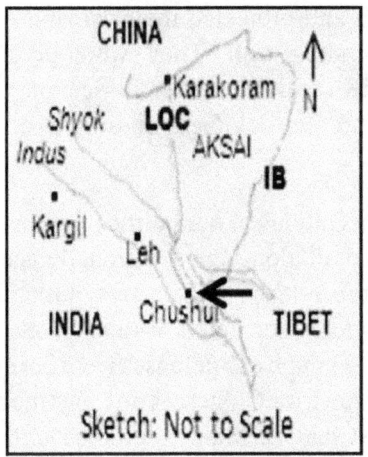

The Indo-Chinese Border in Ladakh runs about 25 Kms East of Chushul Valley. Chushul is a large border village located approximately 150 Kms SE of Leh, the capital town and the most important communication center in Ladakh. Chushul Valley is an undulating, rocky, cold and windy desert. Limited tracked vehicles can move cross-country. The general altitude of Chushul valley is over 14,000 ft. It is dominated by Ladakh Ranges with altitude varying from 5500 m to 6300 m. It is connected by roads and tracks and has an airstrip, which makes this place very important for military operations. Loss of Chushul to enemy would have opened the gateway and a launching pad for the capture of vast strategically vital Indian Territory including Leh.

China had made an unjustifiable claim of over 13,000 sq kms of Indian Territory in NEFA and Ladakh. As a precautionary measure, India had adopted Forward Policy and the Indian Army Units had occupied those tactically important features that were located close to the border. By May 1962, it was evident that the Chinese Army (PLA) units were preparing for a large-scale offensive operations, presumably to capture the territory they were claiming to be theirs. In the summer of 1962, the Chinese troops, in hundreds, crossed the border, surrounded a few of the Indian Army pickets and shouted abuses through public address systems in order to provoke them to start a conflict. Nevertheless, Indian forces kept their cool and refused to be provoked. However, Chinese did not launch any attack and withdrew to their side of the border.

In view of the perceived offensive designs of the PLA, the Indian Army authorities had conceived a plan, worked out the requirement of troops to defend Chushul Area and projected their demand of a division worth of troops for the impending task. They were given only two Infantry Battalions, just one fifth of the demand. Those units were neither trained in High Altitude Warfare nor clothed or armed commensurate to their impending task.

Much against the expectations of our political leaders of that time, the PLA did cross and attacked all along the traditionally accepted Indo - Chinese Border on 19/20 October 1962. Indian Army units that were deployed in small detachments, widely separated from each other, were encircled and attacked by the PLA. Though our defenses were not adequately prepared to face the numerically superior Chinese Army, our men gave a good account of themselves at Chip Chap, Galwan Valley and Demchok. Our Posts had no counter attack capability. Therefore they were overrun one after another.

The heroic deeds and self sacrifices made by men such as, Subedar Sonam MVC, Sepoys Wanchuk, Chiring and Phunchuk both VrC, Major Hasabnis, Subedar Amar Singh, CHM Anand Ram, Hav Tulsi Ram and many more valiant officers and men did prevent the PLA from having a cake walk into Ladakh. Though PLA managed to capture a few pickets, they

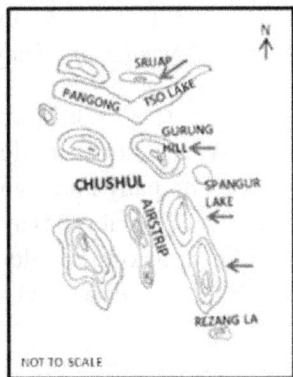

Sketch of Chushul

were forced to slow down their advance towards Chushul. This gave time to our units to improve the defenses in and around Chushul.

Having realized that Hindi-Chini were no more Bhai Bhai, a brigade worth of additional troops were rushed forward to defend Chushul under the command of an able military leader Brigadier TN Raina (later COAS and the High Commissioner of India in Canada) with some artillery support and light tanks. The units got down to prepare their defenses. The high altitude effect on human being (lack of oxygen) and animals combined with sub zero temperature and high velocity wind can have a demoralising effect. Time was running out. The units could not lay mines on all possible enemy approaches. The men were struggling to remain alive and healthy to face the Chinese attack and were doing their utmost. Though not well coordinated, the defenses were ready by the time the Chinese actually launched the attack.

Hills and lakes surround Chushul Valley. The hills dominate the village, airfield and the approaches leading to it. To the North of Chushul is Pengong Tso (A blue fresh water lake that extends deep into Chinese territory) and to the East are Gurung Hill, Spangur Lake and Rezang La (pass). The defense potential of Pengong Tso, Spangur Lake, Gurung Hill and both shoulders of Rezang La were exploited and augmented with troops holding a broad front.

A Company of 1/8 GR was holding Srijap (North of Pangong Tso) under Major Dhan Singh Thapa and the rest of the unit was at Gurung Hill between the two Lakes, which was guarding the NE approach. 13 Kumaon had prepared Rezang La defenses including Magar Hill, which covers the Eastern and SE approach. Major Shaitan Singh was commanding his C Company at Rezang La. Even the God of Mountains could not have chosen any other Company Commanders to lead the men under those adverse conditions other than those two brave officers. They were 'ROCK SOLID'.

At the early hours of 21 October 1962, the Chinese attacked Srijap from more than one direction in waves with their light tanks supporting the attack. Prior to the assault, the Company locality was pounded with heavy shelling. Then the PLA poured in. The Gorkhas at Srijap were prepared for this and repulsed two attacks with heavy casualty on both sides. The only wireless set held by Major Thapa was destroyed in shelling. The post was cut off.

Major Thapa was moving from bunker to bunker encouraging his men to fight and at times, occupying the trench of a wounded or a dead soldier and firing on the attacking enemy. He appreciated that the Chinese will launch a third attack soon, so he rallied his men to be prepared for the glorious martyrdom. The third Chinese attack did come. This time in larger strength including with some tracked vehicles spiting fire and churning the trenches.

Major Thapa, PVC

No help could be expected from outside. The ammunition was running low and there were only a few men left alive. Having left with no other options, wounded and bleeding Major Thapa and his men did what was expected of them. They jumped out of their bunkers with Kukri in their hands and faced the enemy onslaught. It was a hand-to-hand fight to finish. For the Gorkhas who were at Srijap, it was last man, last round. A few seriously wounded and still alive were taken prisoners. The rest were dead except one man who was in a boat in the Lake guarding it. He reached his unit later to tell the story of valour and sacrifice.

Chinese casualty was estimated to be three times more than that of the Gorkhas. After having captured Srijap, the units of the PLA had halted their offensive. This gave the badly needed time for the rest of the Brigade to strengthen the defenses along this approach to Chushul.

Major Thapa was declared dead. However, later he was found in a Chinese POW Camp and was released. He was honoured with PVC for his exceptional bravery against the enemy in battlefield and exemplary leadership beyond the call of duty.

On 18 November 1962, at 0545 hours, after a pause of nearly one month, the PLA units recommenced their offensive and launched a multipronged attack in a broad front from Gurung Hill in the North to Rezang La in the South. After an intense artillery fire, the PLA units contacted the defenses of Gurung Hill held by the brave Gorkhas and Rezang La defended by the C Company of 6 Kumaon. Telephone communication to these localities were cut off. (It could have been due to shelling, but the telephone cables were reported missing, suggesting that the Chinese did cut off the means of communication before launching the attack). An observer from a vantage point had reported the movement of 'sea of Chinese soldiers' in waves advancing towards the defenses. A fresh snowfall during the previous night had improved the visibility of the defenders and they were watching and waiting.

Combined with improved visibility, good fire discipline and intense artillery fire brought down by the field guns of 13 Field Regiment, the Kumaonis and Gorkhas were able to beat back the first wave of attack. The AMX 13 Tanks of 20 LANCERS, played havoc on the enemy by firing from their tanks in manual mode when the automatic loading mechanism froze due to very low temperature. It was Godsend gift to the Infantry thirsting for supporting fire.

By 0900 hours, the Chinese troops contacted the forward posts manned by the Gorkhas and captured a few bunkers. The valiant Gurungs led a kukri charge and retook the positions. Jamedar Amar Bahadur Gurung, the Commander of the forward Platoon, was mortally wounded in the hand-to-hand fight. He was awarded MVC. The artillery unit rose to the occasion and brought down effective fire on enemy. 2/Lt Goswami, 13 Field Regiment who was directing the fire, though lost one of his legs, was awarded MVC for his commendable contribution to the battle till the end. Gunner Gurdeep Singh received VrC and signalers Naik Pritam Singh and Lance Naik Sarwan Singh were awarded Sena Medals. Capt Kher, the Company Commander was wounded. The Chinese were once again forming up to attack when it was decided to move the Company to a tactically more advantageous position and bring down artillery fire (DF SOS) on his abandoned position as and when it is occupied by the Chinese. Thus, the control of Gurung Hill had passed to the attackers. The Chinese had to pay a heavy price and Chushul was still not within their reach. The Kumaonis defending Rezang La were still a hard nut to crack.

The attack on Kumaonis came after a heavy hammering with Recoilless guns and artillery fire on their bunkers. More than 600 Chinese soldiers formed up and launched the attack. C Company 13 Kumaon comprising of 124 officers and men knew what was in store for them and they were ready to do and die. When the Chinese reached the defenses, the Ahirs (mostly from Rewari Dist of Haryana) fought with grim determination for every inch of territory and most of them made their ultimate sacrifice. Several assaults were repulsed. Major Shaitan Singh led his men from the front and was wounded twice. Unmindful of his own safety, Major Shaitan Singh went from post to post raising the morale of his men and continued to direct their firefight, even after being seriously wounded. He refused to be carried to a safer bunker for treatment and died within his Company locality that he was supposed to defend.

Major Shaitan Singh

The ferocity of the battle can be judged from the fact, that out of 124 all ranks, 109 died in action, five seriously wounded were taken prisoner and remaining ten had been evacuated due to serious injury earlier. After the war was over, Major Shaitan Singh's body was recovered with other dead bodies. There was no live ammunition found in the Company. A frozen body with unexploded grenade still in his right hand was the only live grenade recovered from the locality. Once again, it was last man, last round. Major Shaitan Singh was awarded PVC for his supreme valour and ultimate sacrifice. Other gallantry awards to his Company were, eight VrCs and four Sena Medals; a unique in 1962 war. Major Shaitan Singh died a hero, but importantly he lived Hero.

Major-General Ian Cardozo, in his book, 'Param Vir, Our Heroes in Battle', writes, *"When Rezang La was later revisited, dead jawans were found in the trenches still holding on to their weapons... every single man of this company was found dead in his trench with several bullet or splinter wounds. The 2-inch mortar man died with a bomb still in his hand. The medical orderly had a syringe and bandage in his hands when the Chinese bullet hit him... Of the thousand mortar bombs with the defenders all but seven had been fired and the rest were ready to be fired when the (mortar) section was overrun."*

Major Dhan Singh Thapa, PVC and Major Shaitan Singh Bhati, PVC had many things in common. Both were patriots to the core, popular leaders of men and fearless. Most importantly, they were from the Army families, one from Shimla and the other from Jodhpur. They were men of substance. (I realized the enormity of their glorious sacrifice fully when I visited Rezang La and the War Memorial of 13 Kumaon at Chushul to pay my respect. Regrettably, I could not cross over Pangong Tso to visit Srijip.)

On 21 November 1962, the Chinese declared unilateral ceasefire. Thus, the War came to an end. 114 Brigade under Brig Raina was justifiably proud of its conduct in the Battle of Chushul. Outnumbered 10 to 1, they had fought with considerable élan and tactical skills inflicting horrendous casualties on the Chinese. There was no vain sacrifice of lives.

Brig TN Raina

Peking radio admitted to have suffered its worst casualties at Chushul Valley, which was estimated to be over one thousand. The Chinese could not capture their objective; Chushul. 114 Brigade was not defeated. The PLA did not win in this Battle. The task allotted to 114 brigade was to defend Chushul and inflict maximum casualty on the enemy. The Brigade achieved both. Brigadier TN Raina and his men were the winners in the BATTLE OF CHUSHUL. He was decorated with MVC.

India may have come out the second best in the 1962 Indo-Chinese war, but in the Battle of Chushul, Indian Army was the winner.

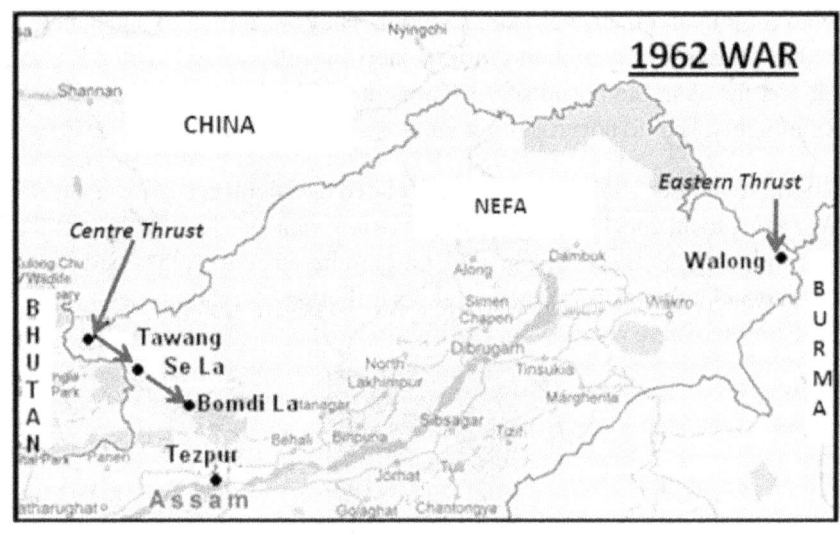

NAMKA CHU - THE KILLING GROUND

*"Forward, the Light Brigade! ... Into the valley of Death
theirs not to reason why, theirs but to do & die...
Then they rode back, but Not the six hundred."*

-Lord Tennyson, the Charge of the Light Brigade,

This is precisely what happened with the Indian Army in 1962 when the Indian Army was ordered to clear Chinese from the disputed Indian Territory in NEFA by the unprofessional politicians. Many professionally competent army generals had analysed and war-gamed the higher directions that they had received from the Govt, asking them to evict the PLA from Thag La Ridge. Some of them were not comfortable with the likely outcome of executing those orders. They expressed their reservations. Not all, but some had represented their views candidly. The politicians did not respect their views. Even though the Army was not prepared for such a war, the directions that were received from the Govt were implemented and the outcome was a DEBACLE.

1962 Indo-Chinese War is also known as DEBACLE in the military circles because, it was an avoidable engagement and one sided aggression that began when the Indian Army was not adequately prepared and ended suddenly and disastrously with humiliating consequences for India. The well-acclimatized and suitably clothed and armed Chinese Army (PLA) had chosen two major thrust lines to advance and capture the disputed areas in NEFA.

Their western thrust line was along Bum La - Tawang Se La Bomdi La. Indian Claim Line in this sector ran north of Thag La Ridge. The Chinese version of McMahan Line included Thag La Ridge in their side of the Border. Thag La Ridge is a watershed, which discharges its water into Namka Chu River, which is fordable at places and dominated by the massive Thag La Ridge by both observation and fire. Major battles were fought in the areas 60 Kms north of Tawang at Namka Chu River Valley. Tawang Town is the road head which is about 200 kms NW of New Misamari; the railhead in Assam. From Tawang, many mule tracks emanate and cross into Tibet through the four prominent passes across Thag La Ridge. Local grazers used seven improvised bridges to take their cattle

Namka Chu Valley

across Namka Chu. They were numbered 1 to 5 from East to West then are Log Bridge and Temporary Bridge.

Khinzemane and Dhola were two Posts that were located on the north and south of the River. The general altitude of the Valley is over 14,000 ft. Fighting in such high altitudes present enormous logistics problems. It is noteworthy, that there were no surveyed maps of this area in 1962.

Because of the militarily nonsensical India's Forward Policy, there were many border skirmishes. On 8 September 1962, a large body of 600 strong enemy forces seized one of the Assam Rifle post. PLA was present on Thag La Ridge in strength, which was estimated to be of a Brigade (PLA Regt). Indian 7 Infantry Brigade that was located at Tawang was ordered to evict the Chinese from Thag La Ridge.

The task given to 7 Brigade had no relationship with its capability. The Brigade, Division and Corps Commanders objected to such a venture against strong PLA forces. They were overruled. 7 Infantry Brigade moved 60 kms from Thawang on foot to Namka Chu Valley and occupied defenses based on the seven Bridges along the River Namka Chu. The River was fordable at places and was dominated from the heights of Thag La Ridge by the Chinese. The defenses were not tactically sound. The Brigade defenses were organized in the killing ground of the PLA, sitting on the Thag La Ridge.

On 8 October, 9 PUNJAB was asked to send a patrol to occupy a high ground on Thag La Ridge. (Charge of the Light Brigade). Major Chaudhry with his Company reached his destination and occupied the firm base. Next day, Chinese attacked Major Chaudhary's position with 20 to 1 superiority. He asked for fire support. It was not given. He was asked to withdraw from there. By that time, the Chinese were already on Major Chaudhary's position and hand-to-hand combat was in progress. Though wounded, he managed to withdraw with what was left of his two platoons. One of his Sepoys, Kanshi Ram, had snatched an AK-47 rifle from a Chinese soldier and carried it with him; probably the first AK 47 Rifle that the Indian Army saw. Naik Chain Singh covered their withdrawal with his LMG until he was gunned down by an enemy machine gun burst. Major Chaudhary who later died of his wounds, Sepoy Kansi Ram and Naik Chain Singh were awarded Maha Vir Chakra for bravery. Two more Vir Chakras were also awarded. The Punjabis lost six dead, eleven wounded and five missing. PLA's casualty as reported by Peking Radio was nearly one hundred dead/wounded.

On 10 October 1962, a strong patrol comprising of one officer and fifty men of 2 Rajput were ordered to occupy one of the passes on Thag La Ridge at 16,000 ft. A battalion of PLA attacked the patrol. Rajputs fought back, but they were overcome with nearly 50% of them dead. The Chinese suffered 33 dead. By 18 October 1962, the PLA had build up to Division strength; mostly armed with AK 47 and supported with artillery in the area of Thag La Ridge. In contrast, Indian Army units were still armed with bolt-action rifles. Ammunition stock was far below the requirement to fight a successful defensive battle. 7 Brigade Commander was unhappy with the defense preparedness. He had shared his anguish with the CO of 2 RAJPUT during one of his visits to the Battalion. The CO replied, "Don't worry Sir, despite their (PLA) superiority, the RAJPUTs won't let you down. If you do get back, see to it that those who got us into this mess get their due". The CO obviously had decided to fight and die there. Such were the leaders of men; 'my country first, my men next, me last'.

By 16 October, additional two Battalions were inducted. Now the Brigade had 9 PUNJAB, 2 RAJPUT, 4 GRENADIERS AND 1/9 GR. By 19 October, it was quite evident that the Chinese had concentrated and were ready for attack.

On the night of 19/20 October, large herds of Yaks were driven through Namka Chu River between Bridge 1 and 5. It was later realized that the Chinese wanted to ascertain the depth of water at their crossing places across the River and also to detonate mines and breach wire obstacles if any. By 5 AM on 20 October, the PLA crossed the River on foot, taking advantage of poor visibility and avoiding the well guarded Bridges. They crossed the river after removing their socks and had worn dry socks after crossing the River. The telephone lines were cut off.

After forming up on the southern bank of the River, they attacked, on a broad front, from the rear (south). Main attack came on 2 RAJPUTS who were defending areas of Bridges 3 and 4, with their defenses facing north. To the shock of the defenders, the attack came from behind. Their trenches were exposed and they had to scramble out of their bunker to face upwards in the opposite direction.

At Bridge 4, 2/ Lt Onkar Dubey with his 7 Platoon, poured fire on the Chinese and broke up two attacks. Later he was severely wounded in the stomach and chest and fell down unconscious. He was taken prisoner. Subedar Dashrath Singh's men turned uphill and opened fire on the advancing Chinese. The Chinese rushed down using cover from tree to tree. Dashrath and his men repulsed three attacks. On the fourth, they came in to hand-to-hand combat. Subedar Dashrath, severely wounded, fell unconscious and was taken POW.

On the eastern flank, Major B K Pant's Company came under heavy attack. The crescendo of AK-47 fire overshadowed the noise of Indian LMGs and rifles. He was a fine example of courage, displayed by the Indian soldier in the war with China in 1962. His company held fast against three waves of Chinese assaults and had suffered heavy casualties. Pant himself was wounded in the stomach and legs. Yet he continued to lead and inspire his men, exhorting them to fight until the end to the last man. The Chinese sensing that the obstacle in taking Rajputs lay with Major Pant, brought a volley of concentrated machine gun fire on his position killing him on the spot. His last words were "Men of the Rajput Regiment, you were born to die for your country. God has selected this small River for which you must die. Stand up and fight like true Rajputs." Then he died shouting the Rajput battle cry; "Bajrang Bali ki Jai."

With the flanking platoons almost wiped out, the remnants fell back to the Battalion HQ. Capt Bhatia, Lt Col Maha Singh Rikh and a few others were now in the Battalion HQ. The Chinese opened up with a machine gun trying to break through the bunkers. When that failed, a Chinese soldier crawled up to the Battalion HQs bunker and threw a grenade just as Lt Col Rikh was peeping out. The grenade hit his rifle and exploded, breaking his jaw and cutting his lips. Lt Bhup rushed out and shot the Chinese soldier and dragged Lt Col Rikh back in. He was propped up and given an LMG to resume firing. Another Chinese LMG burst through the door killed Capt

Bhatia and hit Lt Col Rikh; again on the shoulder. He however, managed to gun down the Chinese soldier. Yet another Chinese soldier broke through the bunker and fired at him in the elbow and leg, consequently breaking them. The pain and loss of blood caused him to collapse. He was taken prisoner.

Lt Bhup continued to hold the enemy off with just one more jawan left alive. The Chinese had now encircled from three sides and were pouring machine gun fire at him. Bhup had no more ammunition to fight. The Chinese threw percussion grenades, overpowered Lt Bhup and the Jawan. Thus, little by little, the superior firepower of the Chinese AK-47s overwhelmed the Rajputs. With ammunition running out, the Rajputs had no chance to contain the onslaught of the numerically superior PLA. Chinese were forming up for third attack. Even the third attack on the depleted Rajput Company was not a cakewalk. Every soldier had to be overcome by hand-to-hand combat. The last few men succumbed to the inevitable.

9 PUNJAB and 1/9 GR on either flanks of 2 Rajputs, suffered similar fate though of lesser degree. 2 Rajput suffered horrendously but lived up to the Regiment's reputation. Of the 513 all ranks, 282 were killed that morning, 81 were wounded and 90 were taken POW without a single round of ammunition left with them to defend themselves. Only 60 men, mostly rear elements got away. 9 PUNJAB had lost 65 dead and 1/9 GR suffered 90 dead. Many more were wounded and captured. 7 Brigade lost a total of 493 men that morning. The Chinese also lost heavily. (Lt Col Rikh who was captured, was subjected to repeated interrogations to find out as to how he motivated his command to fight so bravely under such adverse conditions.)

Thus ended, the Battle of Namka Chu in a debacle. The word 'battle' is grossly misleading; for it was a massacre; a one-sided battle with many Indian soldiers fighting with their last round. The Nation was stunned. Chinese offered to negotiate the issues even after their overwhelming victory. Indian leadership refused and said that there was nothing to negotiate. The remnants of 7 Brigade were ordered to withdraw from Namka Chu and were tasked to defend Tawang; an un-defendable town by a brigade. They suffered these and many more humiliations silently.

In the whole of this tragic episode, there was not a single incident where any of the men questioned or disobeyed an order from his superiors in the battlefield. They all fought to the best of their capability and when there was no other option left, they stood their ground and fell down fighting.

Aye mere waton ke logon Zera ankon men barlo paani
Jo shahid hue hai unki Zara yad karo kurbani.

TAWANG TO BOMDI LA

The famous Chinese philosopher Sun Tzu said, 'if one knows oneself and the enemy, one need not fear the outcome of hundred battles'. With the advantage of hindsight, it appears that Indian leaders; both civil and military of 1962 vintage, neither knew themselves nor the Chinese. Even if they had not known prior to the initial engagements with the PLA, it should have been quite clear by the third week of October 62 that the chances were, for every battle they hoped to win they would lose one hundred; for they neither knew themselves nor the PLA; the enemy.

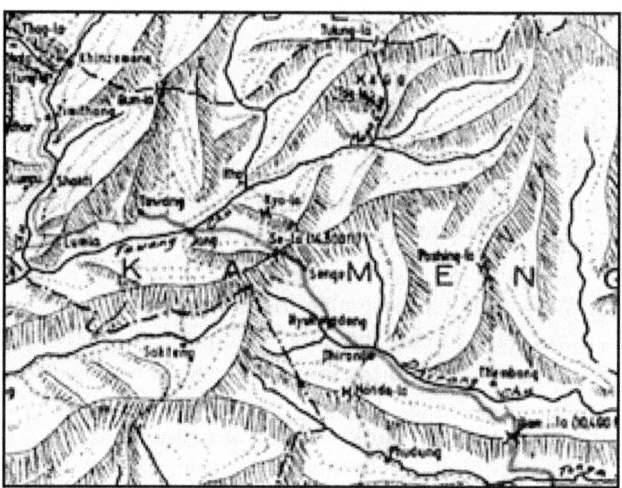

Rd Tawang-Bomdi La

In spite of the hard drubbing at Namka Chu Valley from PLA, Indian leaders wanted to force a settlement of their choice on Chinese rather than opting for a negotiated settlement as proposed by them. The process of negotiation would have gained adequate time to reconsider the Indian claim more pragmatically and build up military capability to defend it. It would have certainly avoided the unnecessary bloodshed and lose of image which India suffered subsequently.

Since India was not willing to negotiate, Chinese decided to attack and evict the Indian Army from NEFA rather than being attacked by India later on (their perception). The advance of PLA units towards Tawang from Namka Chu Valley and Bum La using jungle tracks was more of a large-scale infiltration. En-route, they mostly bypassed or brushed aside the minor opposition offered by the Assam Rifle and Indian Army detachments. The infiltrated PLA units had occupied the hills around the town dominating Tawang.

However, one of the columns of PLA advancing through the IB Ridge south of Bum La met with stiff opposition. This Ridge was held by a platoon of 1 SIKH under an outstanding junior leader; Subedar Joginder Singh with 23 of his brave men. His Commanding Officer knew that the Chinese advancing towards them were numerically superior. Joginder was allowed to withdraw if his Platoon was not able to offer meaningful resistance and cause delay on the enemy. That was an easier option. However, Joginder, the true son of the Punjab adopted the difficult option and decided to stay put. The battle situation was such that the Commanding Officer could not reinforce Joginder's platoon location.

Sub Joginder Singh

Even the knowledge of their certain death for opposing a strong PLA force did not deter Joginder and his men from challenging the superior PLA forces rolling down on them. They decided to teach a lesson to the Chinese for daring to attack a SIKH platoon. The Chinese attacked early in the morning in Waves. The Sikhs repulsed three attacks. Joginder was wounded. Nearly 50% of his men were either dead or wounded. Ammunition was low. He had dispatched three of his men to fetch more ammunition. Even before the resupply of ammunition arrived, fourth attack came from three directions. Joginder knew what was expected of him under these circumstances.

Men came out of the bunkers and hand to hand fight ensued with bayonet and rifle butt. It was last man last round. The three men who went to collect ammunition did not return in time for the final battle. The platoon locality was overrun. Subedar Joginder Singh was seriously wounded and was captured. He died in Chinese custody. Later, he was awarded PVC posthumously; the only PVC in NEFA in 1962. As a mark of respect by one soldier to another, the Chinese later handed over the ashes of Joginder. According to Chinese radio news, PLA had suffered more than 100 men dead in this engagement.

Tawang is an important border town. But It is not suitable to give a stiff defensive battle. The PLA had effectively isolated the Town by occupying all the heights around it. Therefore, troops could not stand up and give a fight at Tawang. They were asked to withdraw on 23 October and move to Se La; a location which is more suitable for fighting a defensive battle.

Many PLA men disguised as local tribal guides had misled Indian Army units into Chinese ambushes. The story goes something like this. Many of the PLA men were working as porters and camp followers in the Assam Rifle and Army posts in disguise for quite some time before 1962 and were familiar with officers and men of the Indian Army and their modus operandi. A few days prior to the outbreak of war, some of them quietly left their job, rejoined their PLA units to act as their guides and directed artillery fire on the Indian defenses.

The subsequent few days were the most traumatic and darkest period in the history of Indian Army. What exactly lead to that chaotic condition will only be known when the reports of the study carried out by two Senior Indian Army Officers are made public. However, even those few critical days were not without some deeds of valor of which every Indian can be justifiably proud of.

4 Garhwal Rifles was deployed ahead of Se La as covering troops to the Brigade Defenses at Nuranang Valley between Tawang and Se La. The Battalion came under attack on 17 November 62. Three attacks in waves were beaten back. Chinese were preparing for the fourth attack when it was decided to capture a Chinese machine gun post which was effectively supporting the Chinese attack. The machine gun was captured by three brave men of 4 Garhwal in an unconventional operation. Rifleman Jaswant Singh Rawat, Rifleman Gopal Singh Gusain and Lance Naik Trilok Singh Negi adopted a most unexpected approach to reach the enemy post from

above the post, slithered down and killed the three Chinese soldiers who were inside with grenades. Rawat literally snatched the machine gun from the hands of the dead Chinese soldier and was crawling back to his own bunker. The hero of the day, Rawat, was killed just before he entered to the safety of his bunker. However, the loss of machine gun had adverse effect on the Chinese fourth attack which was beaten back with heavy casualty.

Rifleman Jaswant Singh Rawat was decorated with MVC and Rifleman Gopal Singh Gusain and Lance Naik Trilok Singh Negi were awarded with VrC. After this, the Battalion was ordered to withdraw from Nuranang which was conducted tactically in an exemplary manner. The CO of the Battalion, Lt Col B M Bhattacharya, was decorated with MVC and the Battle Honour of Nuranang was awarded to 4 Garhwal Rifle.

The outstanding leadership and courage displayed by the Officers and men of 4 Garhwal under adverse conditions was suitably recognized by awarding the unique Battle Honour in 1962. A memorial in honour of Jaswant Singh Rawat has been built. The place is now known as Jaswantgarh. All those passing along the road to Se La pay their respects to the young men who died fighting there in 1962.

To manage the crisis, many Indian Army units were rushed from far-flung areas to NFEA. 4 RAJPUT was one such Infantry Battalion which was rushed from Belgaum to defend Bomdi La. By the time they reached the railhead at Misamari, the 'battle' situation had changed so much that they were diverted to a different task. They were deployed ahead of Bomdi La to defend Dirang Zong. The Battalion had a new Commanding Officer; Lt Col Bramanad Avasthi. His Companies were deployed far away from each other and were constantly harassed by the Chinese infiltrators.

In spite of deeply divided opinion among the senior commanders, the Se La defenses were abandoned without giving any fight and orders were issued to the troops at Se La to withdraw from there and occupy the next line of defenses at Bomdi La.

4 RAJPUT was in an unenviable position. They were tasked to ensure safe passage to the withdrawing forces from Se La. They were in contact with the enemy. This made their task even more difficult. They decided to do it by holding a Bridge, which was a major bottleneck en-route.

Having prepared their defenses, 4 RAJPUT awaited the passing through of the forces withdrawing from Se La. Their locality came under sporadic

Chinese attacks. The troops from Se La never came. Later it was learnt that the troops from Se La had already withdrawn through other routes and were moving towards Bomdi La. Therefore, after destroying those stores that could not be carried with them, 4 Rajput withdrew from their defenses and moved to Lagyala Gompa; an old monastery located on the way to Bomdi La. This had a good defense potential. The CO intended to fight a defensive battle from this place to delay the PLA units and give a clean break to the withdrawing troops. Unfortunately, the Rajputs did not anticipate the presence of Chinese there.

As they were climbing up to the Gompa, they came under heavy fire. Withdrawing under enemy fire was not a viable option. Therefore, Rajputs moved up from different directions. The battle was fierce. Finally, it came down to hand-to-hand combat and after a few hours, the numerically superior Chinese prevailed. All the Rajputs there, including their CO, Lt Col Avasthy were killed or wounded. It was once again "Last man last round". The battlefield was a ghastly sight. Over 200 Chinese bodies and 126 Indian bodies littered the area. A shepherd boy was the only living witness to this heroic episode. (He later became Head Lama of the Gompa). After the cease-fire, the bodies were retrieved. The Commanding Officer's body was found with a letter, written to his wife, in his pocket.

152 Officers/JCOs//Men including the Commanding Officer and Subedar Major of 4 RAJPUT made their ultimate sacrifice. Lt Col Avasthy was commissioned in 2 RAJPUT. (The Battalion, which fought a major battle at Namka Chu Valley.) It is the dream of every Infantry officer to command the Battalion in which he was commissioned. Avasthy was very close to fulfilling that ambition when he was earmarked to take over 2 Rajput. That did not happen. However, his wish was partially fulfilled when he was posted as the Commanding Officer of another RAJPUT Battalion; 4 Rajput, which was also at war with Chinese in the same area.

Due to uncoordinated and indecisive defense plan and confusing command and control set up, the defenders of Bomdi La could not and did not offer any worthwhile resistance to Chinese, when PLA contacted the defenses from many directions including from the South. Indian Army Units could not stand up to the onslaught of numerically superior Chinese multi pronged attacks armed with murderous AK 47 Rifles in the rear areas. Most of the units withdrew to south of Bomdi La to the plains. The Chinese reached as far as Rupa and Chaku south of Bomdi La and posed a threat to Tezpur.

On 23 November 1962 the Chinese had declared ceasefire in all sectors and after a few days they withdrew to their original defenses at Thag La Ridge. Probably the Chinese were surprised by the ease and speed with which they could reach Bomdi La. They were not prepared to fight with such a long axis of maintenance. We will never know why they did this unless the Chinese decide to share the reasons with India.

The speedy advance from Tawang, deep inside NEFA and crossing of the formidable Bomdi La by the Chinese Army units in 1962 had caused panic at Tezpur town, which is located on the Northern Banks of mighty Brahmaputra in Assam. There was no plan to resist Chinese advance South of Bomdi La or to defend Tezpur. Authorities expected the Chinese to knock at the doors of Tezpur soon. Hence, orders were issued to evacuate both civil and military assets from there.

In a grim situation such as this, an anecdote will not be out of place. An Army Engineers unit located at Tezpur was ordered to destroy all the engineering plants and dump them in Brahmaputra River in order to prevent these assets from falling into the hands of Chinese. One among them was a multi-purpose plant which was imported recently. Instead of dismantling and dumping this valuable plant in the River, it was given a deep burial intact. After the war was over (Chinese did not come up to Tezpur) this plant was recovered in serviceable condition and was put to good use. This came to the notice of the local commander. He was very annoyed with the Engineer Officer responsible for not destroying the plant and took him to task for disobedience of orders. I do not know what happened to that officer but that plant survived the wrath of the General and stayed in service for a long time. Such is the rigours of Army discipline. (Do not question the orders; just do...!)

SENTINELS OF WALONG

The Chinese thrust via Tawang was a cakewalk for the PLA and was virtually a debacle for the Indian Army. Simultaneous with the attack in Tawang Sector, PLA crossed the border and advanced towards Walong in the Eastern NEFA. Walong is a small border town of Lohit District in NEFA. It lies on the Western banks of the Lohit River, which is a tributary of the Brahmaputra. It is approximately 20 kilometers South of the Chinese border in the North, roughly the same distance from Burmese border to its East and 180 km by road from Tezu; the district HQ of Lohit. It had an Advance Landing Ground capable of handling light aircrafts. The town is dominated by hills rising up to 10,000 to 16,000 feet MSL in the North and West with their spurs coming down towards the River.

Assam Rifle units were deployed along the border. Although cross border violations were occurring frequently, they were not of serious nature. However, from the early sixties, the nature and frequency of violations had necessitated the deployment of regular Army. Therefore, in March 1962 an Infantry Battalion; 6 Kumaon, was moved and deployed to tackle the Chinese border violations. Their base was at Walong. The heroic battles that were fought for the defense of Walong by this unit including an attack which they launched (the only attack in 1962) on the PLA position between 18 October and 16 November were some of the bloodiest ones in the Indo-Chinese war of 1962.

6 Kumaon under the command of Lt Col CN Madiah was deployed in Kibitu area North of Walong. On the night of October 23, PLA launched a battalion-sized attack on 6 Kumaon. When the Chinese were crossing a bridge, the Kumaonis demolished one end of the bridge. As a result, the attacking Chinese were trapped on the Bridge and were exposed to the effective machine gun fire of 6 Kumaon. Kumaonis killed more than 200 PLA men with accurate fire from close range. Not all was a cakewalk for the PLA. Not being able to launch the attack, the Chinese withdrew. The next attack came from a different direction. This too was repulsed. However, with additional reinforcement, a massive Chinese threat was looming large. Hence, the Kumaonis were ordered to withdraw to Walong main defenses. In the next two days, in addition to 6 Kumaon, 4 SIKH and two companies of 2/8 GR were also flown in, thus making it to a Brigade sector to defend Walong.

On October 24, the Chinese pressed forward their advance towards Walong along the track from the North on the West Bank of the Lohit River and attacked Walong defenses. The Sikhs and Gorkhas repulsed the attack with very heavy causality on the PLA. The Chinese lit the pine trees in the jungle on fire and withdrew behind the cover of smoke. Names of Sepoys Piara Singh and Kewal Singh who fought against both the burning jungle and murderous Chinese automatic fire bravely with total disregard to their safety and made the ultimate sacrifice are etched on the rocky faces of Walong. Kewal Singh was decorated with MVC for his bravery. Having suffered heavy losses, the Chinese halted their advance and established a firm base on the hills overlooking the Brigade Sector. These features were named as Yellow and Green Pimples. The terrain was in favor of Chinese. These features dominated Walong defenses directly by observation and fire.

On 29 October, Brigadier NC Rawley took over the command of the Brigade at Walong. In the mean time PLA had concentrated a division worth of troops between the Border and Yellow and Green Pimples and were sending out small parties to infiltrate into the Walong defended sector to harass by frequent firing, raid and ambush; a well known Chinese Army tactics.

Not wanting to suffer the constant harassment of the PLA, the Brigade commander ordered 6 Kumaon to attack and capture Yellow and Green Pimple areas, which were the source of harassment on 14 November. Kumaonis wanted an extra day to prepare, but it could not be given. Kumaonis attacked with two companies without any artillery fire support. The Chinese retaliated with accurate heavy volume of devastating fire. It was another CHARGE OF THE LIGHT BRIGADE. The fierce attack continued the whole day against very stiff resistance and at the end of the day, a foothold was established. The attack was a partial success. Hand to hand fight ensued with both sides suffering heavy casualties. The ammunition was running low. Strict fire control measures had to be enforced.

To reclaim the lost ground, the Chinese counter attacked Green and Yellow Pimples with greater ferocity. They pressed their attack with human wave after wave coming onto the tenacious hold of the gallant Kumaonis, which was later reinforced with 4 Sikh and Dogras, who also provided the badly needed ammunition to the Kumaonis. Eventually the numerically superior PLA succeeded in evicting the attackers. The Kumaonis, Dogras and Sikhs fell back to their bases; 'NOT ALL, BUT ONLY 50 PERCENT'. In the words of Brigadier (later Lt Gen) NC Rawlley the Brigade Commander, "6 Kumaon fought and fought and fought till there was nothing left to fight.

After this there was an eerie silence" The Battalion was awarded with Battle Honour of Walong and five VrCs.

With the firm hold on Green and Yellow Pimples, which dominated the Brigade Sector, the Chinese commenced their multi pronged attacks on the main defenses of Walong from three directions on 16 November on the Sikhs, Dogras and Gorkhas simultaneously. It was estimated to be more than a Division attack. Both sides suffered heavy casualties. The Chinese, also bypassed the Brigade Defended Sector and established a blockade about five Kms south of Walong in the rear, thus cutting off the route of withdrawal.(another known tactics of PLA)

Sikhs, Kumaonis, Gorkhas and Dogras fought shoulder-to-shoulder and many of them sacrificed their life for the defense of Walong. The Chinese poured in artillery and machine gun fire. At the end of the day, the situation became militarily futile for the Indian Army to fight any longer; hence, orders were issued to withdraw. The left over elements of the Brigade managed to march back through the un-navigated terrain and moved to another Sector in the South.

Then came the news of cease-fire on November 23. The unilateral cease-fire declared by the Chinese brought the war to an end. But many subunits in Walong Sector did not get the orders to cease fire due to lack of communication, hence at many isolated places the fighting continued till the last man had any ammunition left with him.

The Chinese did inflict heavy causality on the Indian troops, but the Sentinels of Walong did not allow the PLA a cakewalk through Walong. **Lt Col CN Madiah,** the Commanding Officer of 6 Kumaon, a thoroughly professional and patriotic Officer was a **'man of steel'**. Even later when taken as prisoner of war (POW) by the Chinese, he kept wearing his Indian Army uniform with badges of ranks and refused all enemy inducements. He was physically abused by the Chinese and lost hearing in one ear and sight in one eye. When repatriated back, he was seen proudly wearing his same tattered olive green uniform.

Near perfect defensive battles were fought for over two months against a numerically superior force and large number of enemy were killed. If destruction of the enemy forces is the aim of defensive battles, it was achieved at the Battle of Walong.

The War Memorial at Walong is etched with the following: ***"The sentinel hills that round us stand bear witness that we loved our land. Amidst shattered rocks and flaming pine we fought and died on Namti Plain".***

PAKISTAN'S FAILED SECOND KASHMIR WAR 1965

Pakistan joined CENTO and SEATO in September 1955. In return, United States pledged to assist the member states economically and militarily. This provided Pakistan an opportunity to strengthen her armed forces at minimal cost. In the period between 1955 and 1965, Pakistan received military aid worth $ 1.5 billion. The equipment included Patton tanks, Saber jets, FI04 Star Fighter aircrafts, M1 rifles, Universal machine guns, mortars, recoilless rifles, guns and every other conceivable type of military equipment.

Chinese aggression on India in 1962 was a setback for Indian image and compelled India to modernize and enlarge her armed forces. Pakistan would have faced a comparatively weaker Indian Armed Forces, had she attempted to annex Kashmir in 1962. However, due to fear of international pressure, Pak did not attempt to annex Kashmir then. By 1965, Pakistanis saw and assessed that Indian Armed Forces are getting stronger and larger day by day. This they could not tolerate. Therefore, they decided to launch the offensive at the earliest with the primary object of capturing Kashmir Valley. However, as part of their strategic deception they initiated the firefight from down South in the Rann of Kutch in Gujarat and expected the Indian Army to react and thin out from J&K before they launched the main offensive there.

In January 1965 the Military Ruler of Pakistan; Field Marshal Ayub Khan, was elected as the president of Pakistan. In order to enhance his political image and be branded as the savior of Kashmir, he decided to find military solution to the long-standing Kashmir dispute. Accordingly, on 9 April 1965, Pak Army launched an attack with their newly acquired mechanized military hardware in the Rann of Kutch to annex the area which they had been claiming to be part of Sind in Pakistan. They captured Sardar Post near Kanjarkot. On 24 April, Pakistan attacked again with tanks and artillery and captured four more posts and the entire Kanjarkot area. Indian Army did not contest with full might at her command. Indian Army neither thinned out from J&K nor put up any major resistance. India expected the forthcoming Monsoon to automatically drive out the Pakistanis from these marshy areas.

Cease fire was declared with the intervention of UK. Ayup Khan and his advisors construed the restraint shown by India to give a fight as weakness on the part of India.

All this time, Pakistan Army was busy in planning and preparation for their second Kashmir Offensive. The primary task of capturing Kashmir Valley was assigned to the Pak Army Divisions guarding the border with J&K. Pak adopted nearly the same strategy in 1965 to capture their objective as they did in 1947. This operation was code named as 'Operation Gibraltar'. It envisaged large-scale guerrilla operations inside Kashmir Valley by a number of guerrilla groups of roughly battalion strength, comprising of trained Pakistan Army personnel, Pakistan Army Special Services Group (SSG) Commando personnel and some Kashmiri militants.

The total strength of the Gibraltar Force was estimated to be anything upto 40,000 men. They were divided into many groups of battalion strength. Salahuddin Force in Srinagar Valley, Ghaznavi Force in Rajauri area, Tariq Force in Kargil area, Babar Force in Naushera and Sikandar Force in Gurais area were operating. Their task was to infiltrate into the rear areas, destroy communication facilities, bridges, logistic installations and military headquarters with a view to create chaotic conditions in Kashmir so that the Kashmiris join the revolt against the Government leading to installation of some pro-Pak leader as head of the State and declare independence or join with Pakistan. The intense Islamic feeling, which was created in 1965 due to the loss of Holy Relic from Hazarathbal, was expected to aid the infiltrators.

The infiltration commenced in August 1965 with large number of well armed and led groups crossing the porous Cease Fire Line from Tithwal in the North to Samba in the South. These men wearing Salwar Kameez moved in small groups and hid themselves outside the population centers. They were in search of guides from among the villagers and Bakarwals living in the remote areas. They were able to infiltrate almost everywhere in the Kashmir Valley, kargil and Leh in Ladakh to carry out sabotage. Many unguarded bridges were destroyed. The road between Jammu and Srinagar and Srinagar and Sonamarg were threatened to be cut off.

After the initial success, the infiltrators found the going getting gradually tough. They faced the major problem of survival. They had to fall back on the local resources for their day today needs. They could not merge with the Kashmiris well. Not all of them spoke Kashmiri language and these men unlike the rice-eating locals, were roti eaters. They dressed up differently. Besides, not all Kshmiris liked the idea of a revolt and bloodshed. Pakistan underestimated the mood of the Kashmiri population and the capability of Indian Army deployed in J&K.

Many Kashmiri locals living in the border areas like the Gujjar boy Mohamad Deen, were not Pakistani sympathizers. They informed of infiltration to the nearest Indian Army units and guided them to the hideouts of infiltrators. They were hunted down by the Army and killed in large number. In Poonch/Rajauri areas where the locals provided some support, they succeeded in establishing foothold. Part of Srinagar was under fire. Though there was no revolt as was expected; they did succeed in creating some confusion and disorder by their acts of sabotage, violence and murder. Poonch Valley was cut off temporarily. This situation warranted immediate large-scale military retaliation.

The Indian Army brought in additional troops into the Valley and the infiltration routes were identified and blocked. Counter infiltration operations were launched inside Pakistan Occupied Kashmir. Fierce battles were fought at Thangdhar, Bugiana Bulge, Sanjoi, Mirpur and at Point 1093 later named as Kumaon Hill.

Pakistanis call 104 Brigade in Thangdhar Valley as Chutney Brigade. It implied that they would make mincemeat out of it. However, in 1965, 1 Sikh made chutney out of Pak posts at Richmar Gali and Pir Sahiba after capturing them. Major Kapoor was awarded VrC. The Battalion was also given the task of destroying a bridge which was used by the infiltrators at Nauseri. It was raining heavily. Before the raid party approached the Bridge, it was destroyed by a lightning strike. The Company Commander observed this. He sent a report to his Battalion HQ, which read as, "Bridge destroyed using lightening provided by God. Mission Successful"

A large number of important pickets were captured in Kargil, across Kishan Ganga River, Uri and entire Hajipir Bulge. Such were the result of the bold reactions of the Western Army commander Lt Gen Harbaksh Singh against the infiltrators that the Pakistani leaders were worried of an impending Indian Army counter offensive against Muzzafarabad town in POK, not far from Hajipir Pass. The Indian Army retook most of the borders posts initially captured by the Pak infiltrators. Their attempt to capture J&K ended with the threat of loss to their own high value territory. The Operation Gibraltor, the second attempt of Pakistan to annex Kashmir, failed to achieve any tangible results due to absence of support from the Kashmiri locals and timely reaction by the Indian Army units.

FORTUNE FAVORS THE BOLD

Having stabilized the situation in J&K after the initial setback caused by the infiltrated Pakistanis in September 65, Indian Army launched a bold counter infiltration operation to trap the infiltrators by blocking their possible routes of ex-filtration. That was not all. Those facilities, which were aiding the infiltrators from deep inside POK, had to be destroyed. Therefore, Indian Armed Forces were permitted to cross the Cease Fire Line and attack inside POK. Hajipir Pass was one such target chosen to be captured.

Hajipir Pass is a vital bottleneck and a road junction, which was used by the infiltrators extensively to provide logistic support to the infiltrators. It was strongly held by the special forces of Pakistan. Capture of this Pass could effectively trap and starve the Pakistani elements inside J&K. It is located inside POK dominating a vast area of Hajipir Bulge; an enclave protruding towards the east. Control over this Pass also provides a direct route via Poonch to Uri and other parts of Kashmir Valley thus improving the connectivity with Uri and Baramula from Poonch and in turn from Jammu.

Hajipir pass is dominated by three hill features namely Bedori in the NE, Sank and Lediwali Gali in the North. Bedori is 14 Km southeast of Uri and Hajipir Pass is 10 km south west of Bedori. It was essential to clear these features before the attackers could reach the pass. The Hajipir Bulge

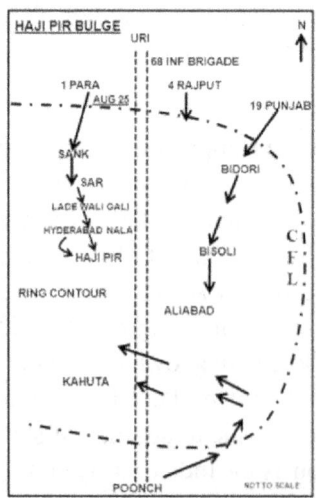

including the Pass itself was held by a brigade worth of troops of Pak regulars and Special Forces.

Indian Army 68 Brigade with additional troops was tasked to capture Hajipir Pass. The operation was code named as OP Bakshi, which was the name of the Brigade Commander. The plan was; 1 PARA Battalion to cross the Ceasefire Line from the west of Uri - Hajipir Track and capture Sank and Lade Wali Gali in Phase 1 by D plus 1, 4 Rajput to pass through 1 PARA and capture Hajipir in Phase 2 by D plus 2. 19 Punjab was to advance from the east of Uri - Hajipir Track, capture Bidori, exploit and link up with 1 PARA. 164 Field Regiment was in direct artillery support throughout the operation.

The multi pronged pincer movement was a brilliant idea to achieve surprise and deception. Hajipir was to be captured by D plus 2. Thereafter, a link up was to take place from the Poonch side by another brigade. The D Day was 25 August 1965.

Surprise and deception was the key to this attack plan. It was planned as a silent attack. To divert the defenders attention elsewhere, a few diversionary attacks were also launched. To ensure success, the attack was launched from two directions. Most of all, the elements aided the attackers to achieve complete surprise with heavy rain and thick fog. This made the going very tough for the attackers, but when the going gets tough, tough gets going. 1 PARA knew this very well.

A Company 1 PARA lead the attack on Sank. Major Ranjit Singh Dayal the Second-in-Command of the Battalion was with the leading Company. Sank had well-fortified strong defenses. The first attack did not succeed. Having been repulsed once, the second attack was launched the next night, with intimate artillery fire support. The Brigade Commander Brig ZA Bakshi was with the leading company. It was raining heavily and it was a difficult climb. The troops reached the top of the feature at 0415 hours next morning.

Major R S Dayal

The enemy was completely surprised and fled leaving behind their heavy weapons including two machine guns and three light machine guns. The Battalion continued its attack beyond Sank without giving the enemy any chance to re-organise and put up a fight. They assaulted the next feature Sar, which is beyond Sank and captured it by 0930 hours August 28. They pressed on and all areas up to and including Ledi Wali Gali were captured by 1800 hours on August 27. The daylight attack stunned the enemy.

4 Rajput had met with unexpected opposition en-route hence, they could not link up with 1 PARA at the appointed time. Major Dayal was keen to exploit the success and pursue the enemy who was on the run. He asked for permission to press on to the Hajipir Pass without giving pause in the battle. Though, all were physically tired, but the success they had achieved invigorated them to go for greater glory,

Permission was granted to exploit the success and maintain relentless pressure on the withdrawing enemy. Major Dayal and his men accompanied by an artillery officer; Capt MD Naidu of 164 Field Regiment resumed their offensive at 1400 hours on August 27.

With wet *shakarparas* and biscuits as ration, Major Dayal led the men down the Hyderabad Nullah towards Haji Pir Pass. The defenders opened fire on them, but an unexpected shower reduced the visibility, hence aimed fire was not effective. As they advanced further, the field guns became out of range. However, the resourceful Naidu did not wait for the redeployment of the guns. He managed to get additional medium gun ammunition allotted and brought down continuous fire on the target. While they were climbing up the slope towards the Pass, the Paratroopers located a house, surrounded it, captured several Pakistanis and recovered weapons from them. Major Dayal disarmed the enemy soldiers and used them as porters before they were taken POW.

On reaching the foot of the Pass, Dayal decided to leave the track and climb straight up, to surprise the enemy. He and his men climbed the difficult hillside under the cover of darkness carrying heavy loads through the rain. By 0600 hours when they had arrived close to the enemy defenses, they came under heavy fire. Leaving the leading platoon and the artillery officer to engage the enemy, Major Dayal took the rest of his men to the west, climbed the western shoulder of the Pass and then rolled down on the enemy from an unexpected flank. The Pakistanis were completely surprised by the daylight attack from the rear. They left their weapons, ran down the hill and escaped. 1 PARA captured the Pass by 1030 hours on August 28.

Capture of Hajipir Pass

The capture of Hajipir Pass was a victory against all odds. While launching the final assault on the pass on August 28, the Paratroopers had to walk up 4000 feet on foot. At times, they even had to crawl on all fours in the slushy mountainside in the night. However, their attack was so well executed that the Pakistani troops left the pass and fled.

Dayal was able to exploit success to an unexpected degree and gave the enemy no time to consolidate themself after the loss of Sank. Relentless offensive action without resorting to classical re-organisation after an attack, kept the enemy off-balance. The enemy could not mount a coordinated counter attack until September 29. By then our troops were able to reorganise on the objective, strengthen their position and beat back the counterattacks.

The most important reason for the success of the operation was unwavering and daring leadership. The command qualities shown by Brigadier Bakshi and Major Dayal were truly outstanding. Their personal example inspired their men to perform great feats of endurance and achieve nearly impossible task. The leadership shown by other officers, JCOs and NCOs was of a very high order too.

The historic capture of Hajipir Pass, in a bold operation by the Indian Infantrymen, is a saga of courage and endurance, which has very few parallels. Concentrated and accurate artillery fire brought down in the form of moving barrage on the targets by Capt Naidu to support the attack, demoralised the enemy and enabled the Paratroopers to close in with the enemy free of any effective interference from the defenders. They did everything the enemy least expected. In recognition of the bravery, bold initiative and leadership provided by Major Ranjit Dayal, he was decorated with MVC. Brig Bakshi was also awarded MVC. Capt MD Naidu was decorated with VrC. Later Dayal retired as Army Commander and was appointed as Lt Governor of Andaman Nicobar Islands and Pondicherry. Brig Bakshi retired as Lt General.

The loss of Hajipir Pass, the principal logistic base of the infiltrators on 28th August and Indian successes in the Krishan Ganga Valley and opposite Uri on 29-31st August 1965 unnerved Pakistan, who assumed that Muzaffarabad was about to be attacked. The supposed liberators of Kashmir were more worried now about POK. It was under these circumstances that the Pakistan Army ordered execution of Operation Grand Slam to threaten and capture Akhnoor with the aim of relieving Indian pressure from J&K.

AKHNOOR WAS THREATENED

With the capture of Hajipir Pass on 28/29 August 1965, the offensive launched by the infiltrators in the Kahmir Valley came to a grinding halt. The Second Kashmir war was heading to a disastrous end for Pakistan. With its fate sealed, the Gibraltar Force disintegrated. Pakistan decided to divert the attention of the Indian Army elsewhere and launched a desperate attack in the Chhamb Sector on 1 September 1965. This operation was code named as 'Grand Slam' with the aim of drawing the reserve forces from the Valley, capturing Akhnoor and cuting off the Poonch Valley. The area selected for the attack by Pakistan regular forces in Chhamb Sector was between River Chenab on the south and Kalidhar Ranges in the north.

191 Infantry Brigade was deployed to defend the area West of Akhnoor up to the Ceasefire Line. The Brigade was also tasked to undertake counter insurgency operations against the infiltrators. On 15 August, the Commander of this Brigade, Brig BF Master was killed in artillery shelling by Pakistan. Brig Manmohan Singh assumed Command of the Brigade. The Brigade had just reorganized its defenses after recapture of five forward posts captured by Pakistan. When Pakistan attacked on 01 September 1965 with an Infantry Division supported with tanks; though the Brigade offered stiff resistance, Pakistan succeeded in capturing Chhamb; a village on the western bank of Manawar Tawi River, in the plains sector.

However, 3 MAHAR held on to its defenses in the hill sector. This unit, though cut off from the Brigade, and without any administrative and artillery fire support, put up very stiff resistance to Pakistan's offensive in the hill sector and foiled its efforts to capture the Kalidhar Ridge in its bid to cut off Akhnoor Rajauri axis at Sunderbani. For fighting a very determined defensive battle, CO 3 MAHAR Col GS Sangha was awarded MVC. Maj Bhasker Roy Who faced the onslaught of Patton tanks with his AMX-13 light tanks and was successful in putting the fear of Indian tenacity in the minds of Pakistanis, was also honoured with MVC.

Lt Col GS Sangha

The Pakistanis had briefly halted the offensive to regroup and cross the Munawar Tawi River. That was also the time when the command of the attacking Pakistan Division was changed to Yahya Khan. They resumed their advance on September third. They attacked Jaurian on September 3rd and took it the next day. By September 5th, they were six miles west of Akhnoor. At this critical stage, the Indian Air Force had resorted to aerial bombardment. This prevented the advance of Pakistani Forces and they failed to capture Akhnoor. It was yet another failure for the Pak Army.

The Western Army Commander planned a strategic counter offensive to Pak's 'Op Grand Slam'. Permission was given to him to attack across the International Border in the Punjab and south of it. On 06 September, our Forces crossed the IB and launched a full-fledged offensive in three sectors in the Punjab and they were heading for Lahore. On 08 September another offensive was launched in Sialkot Sector forcing the Pak Army to commit its reserves in a desperate attempt to save Pakistan. This unexpected large scale counter offensive operation launched by the Indian Army compelled Pakistan to withdraw part of its forces from the Akhnoor Sector. Thus, the scene of action had shifted from Akhnoor Sector to Lahore. The initiative now shifted to Indian Army. Operation Grand Slam therefore failed as the Pakistan Army was unable to capture Akhnoor and cut off the Akhnoor Rajauri axis ; it became one of the turning points in the war when India decided to relieve pressure on its troops in J&K by attacking Pakistan further south across the IB in Punjab.

During the initial stages of Operation Grand Slam, Pakistan army had surreptitiously infiltrated and occupied some Indian Territory on the Kalidhar Ranges in general area Pt 3776, which was not occupied by us. This intrusion had to be cleared and Pak forces had to be pushed back behind the Cease Fire Line.

6 Sikh LI and 1 MADRAS were ordered to clear the enemy from these positions. The 6 SIKH LI assaulted and captured two of their objectives. The enemy brought down heavy artillery fire and counter-attacked three times. Two of the counter-attacks were beaten off with heavy casualties to the enemy. Due to heavy casualties and pressure of the enemy, our troops had to fall back from one of the two hill features.

After a brief halt on the night of 3 October 1965, the Battalion was given the task of clearing the same objective with some additional troops. On 4 October 1965, 6 Sikh LI secured it objectives after climbing a steep slope. Despite casualties and strong opposition, our troops continued to press forward and successfully secured three other important features by the evening of the same day. The enemy counter-attacked, but it was repulsed with heavy casualties.

Despite heavy casualties and fatigue, Trig Point 3776 was finally cleared of the Pakistani intruders by mid-day 5 October 1965. In this action, the Battalion displayed remarkable courage, determination and self-sacrifice for which the Commanding Officer, Lt Col PK Nandagopal, was awarded Maha Vir Chakra. Two Vir Chakras, four Sena Medals, five Mention in Despatches and one COAS's Commendation Card were also awarded. Thus ended the operation Grand Slam in which Pak Army failed for the second time in J&K to cause any major damage. Now the focus was at Lahore.

MARCH TO LAHORE

After the Pakistan's attempt to capture Akhnoor, it was decided to treat this as an act of aggression hence, a decision was taken to launch a limited offensive in Sialkot and Lahore Sectors with our I and XI Corps. Accordingly, 15, 7 and 4 Divisions of XI Corps were tasked to advance and capture areas upto Ichhogil Canal. The Icchogil canal runs north south, parallel to the border for about 70 miles from the River Ravi to the River Sutlej. This canal is a protective moat about 140 feet wide and about 15 feet deep. It has a high steep cement concrete sidewalls and strong fortifications along its embankments with pillboxes and gun emplacements. Though built in the name of irrigation, its primary aim was to be an obstacle to protect Lahore. It is a formidable obstacle, both for the tanks and infantry.

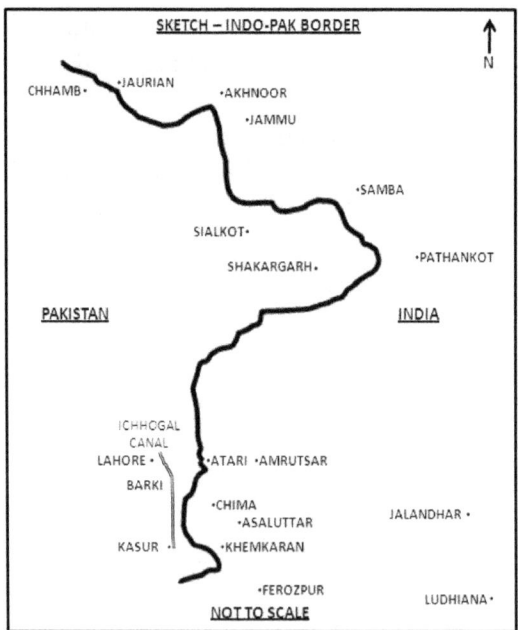

On the sixth of September 1965, the Indian Army crossed the IB on the Lahore-Kasur sector at three places each with a Division supported by tanks. By the evening on the same day, 15 and 7 Division troops had advanced up to the east bank of Ichhogil canal after having over run Burki Village and were at the outskirts of Lahore. Pakistan Army units were holding the major bridges over the Ichhogil Canal in strength and blew up those it could not hold. Therefore, no attempt was made to cross Ichhogal Canal.

However, 3 JAT under the inspiring leadership of their Commanding Officer Lt Col Desmond Hayde had crossed the Ichogil canal and captured the town of Batapore west of the Canal. Pak Air attack was directed towards 3 JAT. In the air attack, 3 JAT did suffer some casualties, but held on to their position on the western side of the Canal. Ammunition and stores vehicles were taking bulk of the damage.

The higher headquarters had no information that 3 JAT had captured Batapore and that they were on the western Bank of the Canal. Presuming that 3 JAT was on the near Bank of the Canal, orders were issued to 3 JAT to withdraw from there. The withdrawal of 3 JAT was a serious setback and Lt Col Desmond Hayde; the CO, was disappointed. However, Dograi was eventually captured by 3 JAT on 21 September and held against violent counter attacks. The CO of 3 JAT was decorated with MVC for his excellent command performance throughout the operations and personal courage and exceptional qualities of leadership shown by him.

Lt Col D Hayde

In the south, the advance of 4 Division was stalled by Pakitani reactions. Later, Pak Forces launched a counter offensive with their 1 Armoured Division and captured Khem Karan. 4 Division was ordered to withdraw and was tasked to occupy defenses at Chima, Valthoha and Asal Uttar.

On the morning of Sept 8, Pakistan launched a counter offensive in Khem karan Sector with their 1 Armoured Division. Their mission was to secure the line of River Beas to a point beyond the bridges on GT road by the evening of September 9. After the initial probing attacks, further advance was delayed due to lack of administrative support. During this pause in the battle, Asal Uttar was reinforced. Enemy tank runs were identified and were flooded with canal water at selected places with a view to stall the Pakistani Armoured Thrust.

On September 10, when the Pak Forces resumed the advance, they encountered very strong opposition and the flooded area proved to be the graveyard of many Pakistani tanks. Decan Horse gave a very good account of themselves. Some of the toughest tank battles of this war were fought here. The CO of the Regiment, Lt Col AS Vaidya was awarded MVC. He was to achieve many more glories in the later part of his life. Pakistani tanks were nearly immobilized. What followed at Asal Uttar lead to decimation of Pak 1 Armoured Division. Its GOC was wounded and the senior most artillery officer was killed.

4 Grenadiers which was deployed in the general area of Chima village was sited to guard the northern approach to Asal Uttar. At 0800 hours on 10 September 1965, Pakistani forces launched an attack with a regiment of Patton tanks on 4 Grenadiers. Intense artillery shelling preceded the attack. The enemy tanks penetrated the forward position by 0900 hours. Company Quarter Master Havildar Abdul Hamid who was commander of an RCL gun detachment, moved to a flanking position with his gun mounted on a Jeep under intense enemy shelling and tank fire. Taking up a tactically advantageous position, he knocked out the leading enemy tank and then swiftly changing his position, he sent another tank up in flames. By this time the enemy tanks in the area had spotted his jeep and brought his jeep under concentrated machine-gun and high explosive fire. Undeterred, Abdul Hamid fired on a yet another enemy tank with his recoilless gun and destroyed the third enemy tank. Before he could change his position, an enemy high explosive shell mortally wounded him.

CQMH Abdul Hamid

Abdul Hamid is credited with the destruction of a total of seven Pakistani tanks in the entire battle, out of which, three tanks were destroyed at Asal Uttar in one engagement by his bold and masterly employment of his jeep mounted RCL gun.Havildar Abdul Hamid's brave action inspired his comrades to put up a gallant fight and to beat back the heavy tank assault by the enemy. His complete disregard for his personal safety during the operation and his sustained acts of bravery in the face of constant enemy fire were a shining example not only to his unit but also to the whole Division and were in the highest traditions of the Indian Army. Company Quarter Master Havildar Abdul Hamid was honoured with the highest wartime gallantry award, Param Vir Chakra, posthumously.

The award was presented to his spouse, Shrimati Rasoolan Bibi by Dr Sarvepalli Radhakrishnan, the then President of India during the 1966 Republic Day Parade. Abdul Hamid was born in a Muslim Darzi family at Dhamupur village in Ghazipur District of Uttar Pradesh on July 1, 1933. His father Mohammad Usman was a wrestler. Abdul Hamid was enrolled into The Grenadiers on 27 December 1954. He was later posted to 4GRENADIERS. During the Sino-Indian War of 1962, Hamid's Battalion participated in the battle of Namka Chu against the Chinese. After five years of service in the anti-tank platoon, Abdul Hamid was promoted and given charge of quartermaster stores of his company. As he was the best firer of RCL gun in the Battalion, he was reverted back to the RCL platoon just before the war.

In his memory, a mausoleum was constructed on his grave by the 4 Grenadiers at Asal Uttar and each year a mela is held on the date of his martyrdom. There is a dispensary, library and school in the name of CQMH Abdul Hamid in Asal Uttar village.

In this Battle, 97 Pak tanks were destroyed or damaged. 72 of them were new Patton Tanks. 32 Tanks were captured in serviceable condition. 12 Pak officers and seven men had surrendered. After the War, a tank cemetery was created at Bhikkiwind, now known as Patton Nagar.

Patton Nagar

On 8 September 65, our Forces (1 Corps) crossed the IB in Sialkot sector and advanced up to Chawinda and Phillorah with a view to capture and isolate Sialkot. Pakistani Air Force was active and the attacks caused moderate damage to the tank columns. Our Forces continued their attacks on 10 September with multidirectional assaults and succeeded in pushing the Pakistani forces back to their base at Chawinda, where they were stopped. A Pakistani counterattack at Phillora was repulsed with heavy damage, and the Pakistanis settled in defensive positions. However, the Pakistani situation improved as reinforcements of two independent brigades from Kashmir arrived. Pak committed her strongest strike element,1 Armoured Division. They managed to repulse Indian attacks on Chawinda.

Two days after the offensive started across the IB opposite Lahore, another front was opened opposite Sialkot. The aim was to capture the Grand Trunk Road around Wazirabad, thus completely cutting off Pakistani supply line to Sialkot. Realising the threat, Pakistanis rushed two regiments of their 6 Armed Division from Chhamb to the Sialkot sector. Some of the largest tank battles in history, since the Battle of Kursk in World War II, were fought here.

Lt Col Tarapore

On 11 September 1965 17 (POONA) HORSE was tasked to attack on Phillora in the Sialkot Sector. Brave Lt Col Tarapore commanded the Regiment. He was with the leading tanks between Phillora and Chawinda. In the face of heavy opposition from the Pakistani tanks, Lt Col Tarapore held his ground and gallantly attacked Phillora under intense enemy tank and artillery fire. He was wounded, but he refused to be evacuated. He led his regiment to capture Wazirwali on 14 September and Jassoran and Butur-Dograin -Di on 16 September 1965.

Though his own tank was hit several times, he maintained his pivots at both these places and thereby helped the supporting infantry in its attack on

Chawinda. Inspired by his leadership, the regiment fiercely fought the enemy armour and destroyed approximately sixty Pakistani Army tanks, suffering nine tank casualties. At the thick of the battle, Lt Colonel Tarapore's tank was hit and was enveloped in flames. He died a hero's death. The valour displayed by Lt Col AB Tarapore in this heroic action which lasted six days, was in keeping with the highest traditions of the Indian Army. Lt Col A B Tarapore went down fighting on board his Centurion tank and was recognised as the bravest of the braves in battle.

Lieutenant Colonel Ardeshir Burzorji Tarapore was awarded with the highest wartime gallantry medal, Param Vir Chakra, posthumously for his outstanding leadership and bravery of exceptional order.

Ardeshir Burzorji Tarapore was born on August 18, 1923 in Mumbai. He belongs to the family of General Ratanjiba, who led the army of Chatrapati Shivaji Maharaj. He was awarded 100 villages of which Tarapore was main village. The name Tarapore comes from this village. He did his schooling at Sardar Dastur Boys' Boarding School, Pune. He completed his matriculation in the year 1940. After schooling, he applied for the army and was selected. He did his training at the Officers' Training School at Golconda and was commissioned in the 7th Hyderabad Infantry (State Force) as a Second Lieutenant.

He was popularly known as "Adi". Adi was not very happy joining the infantry; instead, he wanted to join an armoured regiment. When his battalion was inspected by Major General El Edroos, the Commander-in-Chief of the Hyderabad state forces at the grenade throwing range, due to an accident, a grenade fell into the bay area. Adi was quick to jump and throw it away. However, the grenade exploded in the mid-air, which left him injured as the flying shrapnel hit his chest. Major General Edroos, was a witness to this event which kept him spellbound. He was impressed by the exemplary courage displayed by Ardeshir. Major General Edroos summoned Ardeshir to his office and congratulated him for his efforts. Ardeshir took this opportunity and requested that he be transferred to an armoured regiment. The General accepted this and he was transferred to the 1st Hyderabad Imperial Service Lancers.

Later, when Hyderabad merged with Union of India, this unit was also eventually amalgamated with the Indian Army. Ardeshir was shifted to Poona Horse and was commissioned on 1 April 1951. He rose to become

Commanding Officer and commanded his very own regiment; Poona Horse in the 1965 war against Pakistan.

In the same area Major Bhupinder Singh of Hodson's Horse led his squadron with distinction in the battle of Phillora and Sordreke in Pakistan between 11 and 19 September 1965. With skilful deployment and bold action, his squadron was able to cause large-scale destruction of Pakistani tanks. Although his tank was hit on several occasions, he continued to remain in effective command and by several acts of personal gallantry inspired his men to fight courageously. On 19 September in the battle of Sordreke his tank was hit and caught fire. While abandoning the tank he was burnt severely and subsequently died. For his inspiring example of personal sacrifice and bravery in the best traditions of the Indian Army he was decorated with MVC.

On 22 September, the United Nations Security Council unanimously passed a resolution that called for an unconditional ceasefire from both nations. The war ended the following day. At the end of hostilities on 23 September 1965, India held about 200 square miles (518 square kilometers) of Pakistani territory in the Sialkot sector including the towns and villages of Phillora, Deoli, Bajragarhi, Suchetgarh, Pagowal, Chaprar, Muhadpur, Tilakpur south east and east of Sialkot city, which were returned to Pakistan after the Tashkent Declaration in January 1966. Likewise, Pakistan handed over up to 1,600 Square miles of Indian Territory of which 1,300 square miles were in the desert sectors.

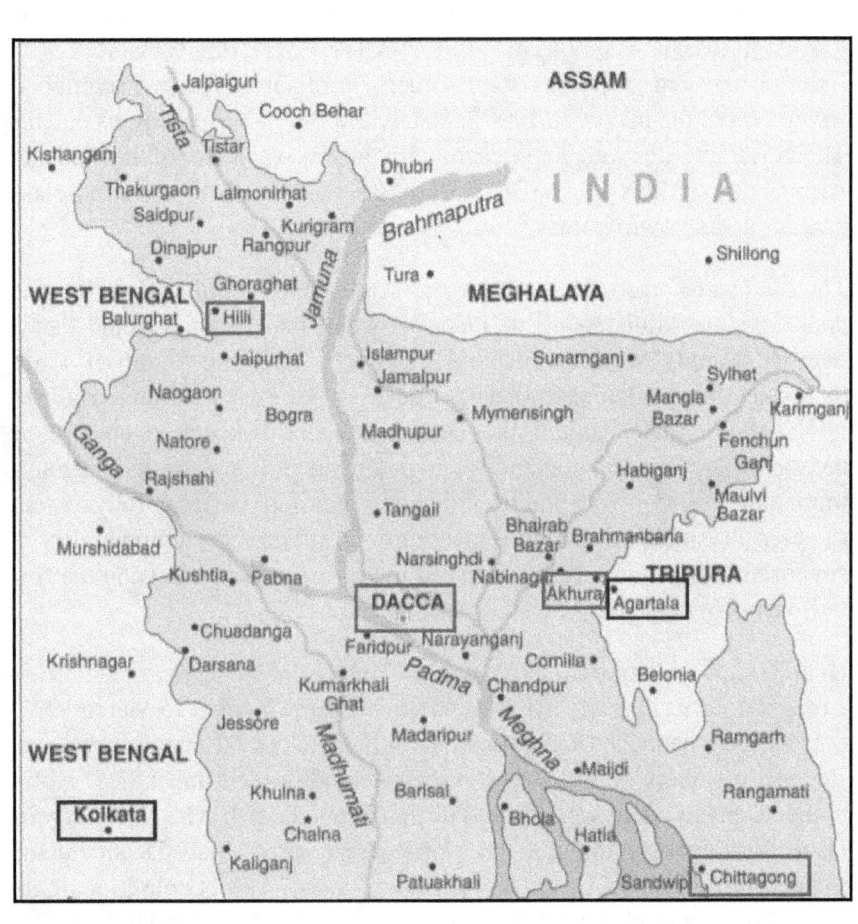

WAR OF LIBERATION

The partition of India in 1947 was one of the greatest tragedies of Indian history. Hundreds of thousands of people were violently killed in both civilian and military clashes. The newly created state of Pakistan was located in two blocks thousands of kilometers away from each other with India in between. West Pakistani leaders (stronger of the two segments) never treated the people of East Pakistan, the Bengali Muslims, as equals. Their civil liberties were suppressed with the muscle power of the Pakistan Army. For over 20 years, the Bengalis of East Pakistan lived as second-class citizens in their own country.

The final straw was when their elected leader Shiek Mujibur Rehman was denied Prime Ministership of Pakistan when his Awami League Party, overwhelmingly won the general elections. The imposition of Urdu language and the denial to their political parties their legitimate right to governance, finally united the people of East Pakistan against their dictators. They made a demand for an independent Bangladesh. Pakistan's immediate reaction was one of violent suppression. General Yahya Khan the then President of Pak, in a meeting with his military commanders is supposed to have said, "Kill three million of them (Bengalis) and the rest will eat out of our hands".

Gen Tikka Khan, notoriously known as "Butcher of Bengalis, executed his barbaric orders ruthlessly in letter and spirit. On the night of 25 March 1971, the Pak Army launched 'Operation Searchlight' to crush Bengali resistance. Bengali members of military services were disarmed and killed. Able-bodied Bengali males were picked up and gunned down. The University of Dacca was attacked and hundreds of students were killed. Death squads roamed the streets of Dhaka, killing more than 7,000 people in a single night. Within a week, nearly 30,000 people had been killed and their bodies thrown in rivers. Chittagong lost half of its population.

Over ten million refugees came to India creating serious strain on the resources. It forced the Indian military to intervene to prevent further exodus of refugees and save the people of East Pakistan from genocide by their own Army. Meanwhile, the Pak Army arrested Sheik Mujibur Rehman, the elected leader and Presidential candidate. Left with no other option, the leaders of Awami League Party declared Independence and renamed their country as Bangladesh on 10 April 1971. The Mukti Bahini, the Army of Bangladesh was formed to confront the Pak Army.

Because of their intimate knowledge of the terrain and training in guerrilla warfare tactics, Mukti Bahini, with the support of Indian Army, had caused serious concern in the minds of the generals of Pakistan. To divert the attention of the Indian Armed Forces from the East, Pakistan attacked across Indian's Western border. Pakistani Air Force launched multiple attacks on the Indian Air fields on 03 December 1971. Indian Prime Minister Mrs. Indira Gandhi declared war on the same day on Pakistan; both in the East as well as in the West. General Manekshaw (later Field Marshal), the then Army Chief was given the mandate of liberating Bangladesh with the Army, Navy and Air Force. The plan was to bypass strong oppositions, converge and capture Dhaka at the earliest.

PM Indira Gandhi and Sam Manekshaw

There were many strong and well organized defended areas inside East Pakistan between the International Border and Dhaka. All could not be bypassed. Many intense battles had to be fought by the units of the Indian Army before they could reach Dhaka. The Battle for Hilli was one such battle which was most severely contested by Pak Army. The loss of Hilli would have cut off the entire Northern enclave of East Pakistan. The fighting started here well before the declaration of war on 3 December and continued even after the surrender of Pak Army on 16 December.

The commander of the Pakistani 205 Infantry Brigade, Tajamul Hussain Malek (the only Brigadiers out of 32 of them in the East Pak to be promoted to the higher rank later) who was responsible for the defense of Hilli, fully utilised the unlimited forced free labourers from local population, to build a strong defensive positions and had created many strong screen positions on all the approaches to Hilli. After the war ended, it was revealed by the locals, that most of the Bengali workers, on completion of their work were massacred and their bodies either cremated secretly or thrown into rivers for security reasons.

8 GUARDS, was tasked to capture Morpara; an important defended area outside Hilli. After a heavy fight and loss of lives, the unit established a foothold into the Pak defenses. 2/Lt Shamsher Singh Samra was leading the assault. Enemy machine gun fire hit him. Regardless of his injury, he closed in with the enemy, assaulted the enemy position with a grenade and pulled the pin out of another grenade to throw when he was hit again. He died with the second grenade still clutched in his hand.

Lance Naik (L/NK) Ram Ugrah Pandey, a fearless hero cleared two bunkers one after another by his tenacious offensive action and helped his Company to maintain the momentum of attack. Before he could destroy the third bunker with a rocket, he was hit by gunfire and died on the spot. The Battalion captured their objective albeit at a heavy price; 60 killed, 79 injured including four of the company commanders; a shining manifestation of officers leading from the front in war. 2/ LT Samsher Singh Samra and L/NK Pandey were decorated with Maha Vir Chakra posthumously for their exceptional bravery and sacrifice. Their Commanding Officer Lt Col Shamsher Singh was awarded the third Maha Vir Chakra for his outstanding leadership in the face of the enemy.

10 Mahar was part of 81 Mountain Brigade under 8 Mountain Division which was tasked to capture Sylhet town from the East. The General Officer Commanding of the Division, Maj Gen KV Krishna Rao (later COAS) also from the Mahar Regiment had considered four major approaches to capture Sylhet. Finally, he decided to adopt the longer and the least expected approach from the South. Accordingly, 10 Mahar acting as advance guard, commenced their advance from Shamshernagar towards Maulvi Bazar on 8 December 71. This town was strongly defended with minefields all around. The Brigade Commander decided to launch an attack and capture Maulvi Bazar.

10 Mahar was tasked to capture a Tea factory at Chatlapur which was a part of the Brigade objective. The Battalion advanced towards the Tea Factory

and came under heavy machine gun fire from the Tea Factory Managers Bungalow. Further advance was held up. The CO decided to infiltrate a small party to neutralize the machine gun fire before launching the attack.

Sepoy Ansuya Prasad volunteered to participate in the raid. He was selected along with a few others. He took some additional grenades and advanced towards the Bungalow. While closing in, he suffered a bullet injury at his leg. Undeterred by the injury he sustained, he crawled further and noticed that there was a store room at the rear side of the Bungalow which was being used to stock ammunition. He crawled further towards the ammunition store and once again, he was shot at his shoulder. With total disregard to the bleeding and his personal safety, he reached the ammunition store and lobbed a grenade. The ammunition store exploded with a big bang and the whole Bungalow was in flame. Later, 10 burned bodies were found with helmets. 10 Mahar captured the Tea Factory. Subsequently Sylhet was encircled by 8 Mountain Division. The two Pak Brigades which were defending the town surrendered on 17 December 71.

Sepoy Ansuya Prasad succumbed to his injuries. He had just 11 days of service with the Battalion. For his exceptional bravery beyond the call of duty, he was decorated with MVC posthumously. Anuya Prasad, son of Sri Dayanand was born at village Nanna in Chamoli District of Garhwal on 19 May 1953. He was the youngest recipient of MVC in 1971.

UNIQUE PARAMVIR ALBERT

14 GUARDS was tasked to capture a East Pakistani position at Gangasagar, near Akhaura (about 6 kms from Agartala). This was an important rail link to Dacca. It was a well-fortified position. 14 GUARDS, which was located at Agartala in Tripura, after crossing the border from the East, launched the attack on an enemy locality at 0400 hours on 4 December 1971. L/Nk Albert Ekka, an unassuming and brave lad belonging to Uraon Tribe from Jari village, Ranchi district of Jharkand, was part of the left forward attacking company of the Battalion.

L/Nk Albert Ekka

The Company came under intense artillery shelling and heavy small-arms fire. The assault was held up by a light machine gun (LMG) fire from a well-fortified bunker and had inflicted heavy casualties. Albert volunteered to silence the enemy LMG. With total disregard to his personal safety, he closed in with the enemy and charged and killed the enemy and silenced the LMG. He was wounded in this encounter, but he continued fighting with his section and had covered distance of 1.5 km clearing the opposition en-route.

His platoon had almost accomplished the objective assigned to it when a medium machine-gun (MMG) opened up from the second storey of a well-fortified building. It was inflicting heavy casualties and holding up their further advance. Once again, Albert, despite his serious injury and under heavy fire, crawled forward until he reached the building and threw a grenade killing one enemy soldier and injuring the other. However, the MMG was still firing. Albert, with complete disregard to his safety and beyond the call of duty, climbed over the side wall, entered the bunker from behind, bayoneted and killed the enemy soldier manning the MMG, thus silenced the weapon.

In the process of attack, this lad had sustained more injuries and died of excessive bleeding due to multiple injuries. With his personal sacrifice, he saved his Company from suffering more casualties and ensured success in their task. For this act of exceptional bravery beyond the call of duty and the supreme sacrifice of his life, he was awarded Param Vir Chakra; the only PVC awarded in the Bangladesh Liberation War. Gangasagar was captured by 14 GUARDS. Now, the Southern and South Western flanks of Akhaura were wide open. Akhaura was captured subsequently and thus paved the way to the great 'March on to Dhaka'. Brig Sant Singh MVC and his Brigade made a dash to Mymansingh and captured in a record time. A Bar was added to Brig Sant Singh's MVC which was awarded to him in 1965 for his inspiring leadership and command performances.

The people of his town honoured Albert Ekka by naming a major Road Junction at Ranchi, as Albert Ekka Chowk with a life size statue of Albert prominently positioned on a high pedestal in a beautifully designed memorial. In 2000, on the eve of 50th Republic day, Government of India issued a postal stamp in his memory. His wife, Balamdeen Ekka and his son Vincent Ekka survive him.

With the total destruction of Pak Air force in the East and the blockade of the sea by the Indian Navy, the Indian Army and Mukti Bahini was able to reach Dhaka and achieve a total success of the plan made by General Manekshaw. Bangladesh was liberated on 16 December 1971. Pak Army in the East surrendered at Dhaka. 93,000 prisoners of war were taken.

Surrender Ceremony

Nearly three million Bengalis were killed in this war. However, those who remained alive could breathe the air of freedom they sought for over 20 years. They were no more second-class citizens in their own country. Their dream of their SONAR BANGLA was achieved through the ultimate sacrifices of brave heroes like Albert Ekka, Shamsher Samra, Anusuya Prasad, Pandey and many more from the Indian Army.

HOSHIAR SINGH AT BASANTAR

In December 1971, with the war going well for India in the East, Pakistan was desperate to divert the Indian resources from the east. To achieve this, Pak Army activated India's Western Border and captured a few tactically important features. To prevent further ingress into Indian Territory, India decided to launch a counter offensive through Shakargarh Bulge and eliminate any threat to the strategically important Pathankot - Jammu Highway, which was the only major lifeline connecting Pathankot with Jammu and beyond to Srinagar Valley at that time.

India's border with Pakistan in the West is not a linear one. There are bulges (protrusions) in the International Border on both sides. The Bulge opposite Shakargarh; a small border town in Pakistan, is into the Indian side. It is known as Shakargarh Bulge. The border here is 5 to 10 miles to the Pathankot - Jammu Highway. Any intrusion or loss of this Highway would endanger the maintenance of the entire Jammu and Kashmir. The terrain here in general is dotted with small villages and criss-crossed with seasonal rivers on both sides of the border. Artificial embankments were added to the riverbanks and the area close to Border was prepared to conduct military operations with bunkers and mine fields on both sides to prevent a free run of each other's mechanised forces.

The Indian counter offensive commenced with tanks and infantry advancing into the Shakargarh Bulge from the North-East and established a foothold across the Basantar River after a few strongly contested skirmishes between the International Border and the line of River Basantar. The Armoured Brigade commanded by Brig AS Vaidya MVC spearheaded the advance and reached Basantar River. As was expected, the reaction from the Pakistan Army to eliminate the build up across the Basantar River was very swift. Pakistan used heavy artillery, tanks and infantry to push the Indian forces behind Basantar River. The bridgehead was held and was being enlarged by 3 GRENADIERS, 6 MADRAS and 16 MADRAS with a Squadron of 17 POONA HORSE against the onslaught of the Pakistan Army.

Major Hoshiar Singh

The 3 Grenadiers continued the assault against violent reaction from the enemy and captured their objective by 16 December. The enemy bunkers were cleared after fierce hand-to-hand fighting. Major Hoshiar Singh was the commander of C Company; the left forward company, which faced the major brunt of counter attack. Unmindful of the enemy shelling and tank fire, he went from trench to trench, encouraging his men to remain steadfast and fight. Inspired by his courage and leadership, his company repulsed many counter attacks. Casualties were heavy on both sides. On December 17th, the enemy mounted yet another attack in battalion strength with heavy artillery in support. An enemy shell landed near one of the medium machine gun post and injured the crew. Major Hoshiar Singh, though he himself was wounded, rushed to the machine gun pit and operated the gun inflicting heavy casualties on the attacking enemy. The enemy attack was repulsed, and they beat a hasty retreat leaving behind 85 dead, including their Commanding Officer - Lieutenant Colonel Mohammed Akram Raja and three other officers.

Throughout this operation, Major Hoshiar Singh displayed conspicuous gallantry in the face of the enemy with grim determination and indomitable spirit. His dogged resistance, complete disregard to his personal safety and cool courage so inspired his command that they performed outstanding acts of gallantry and defeated enemy's attempts to destroy the bridgehead. The steadfastness and dauntless courage displayed by Major Hoshiar Singh were in keeping with the highest traditions of the Army and his continued performance of his duty despite serious wounds was an act beyond the call of duty. For his sterling performances in war, he was honoured with the highest wartime gallantry award, Param Vir Chakra.

Before they finally disengaged from the Bridgehead, the last of the Pakistani tanks left in the bridgehead and the only tank of 17 POONA HORSE, fired at each other simultaneously. The outcome of this fatal engagement is yet another story of courage and dedication to duty out of all proportion. The Armoured Brigade Commander was awarded Bar to his MVC for his brilliant leadership and bravery in the face of the enemy.

The names of Major Hoshiar Singh and 2 Lt Arun Khetarpal of the Indian Army and Lt Col Akram Raja of the Pakistan Army and many more who were involved in the Battle of Basantar will remain engraved in the military history of both countries, for they were the heroes of this historic Battle. The bridgehead was one of the largest graveyards for the tanks including the Patton Tanks comparable only to Longewala, in this War. 66 Pakistani tanks were destroyed and 20 were captured intact. The bridgehead across the Basanter River was saved and Pakistan Army was defeated once again.

SHAHEED ARUN KHETARPAL

Arun Khetarpal (Arun) was the son of an Army Officer born on 14 October 1950 at Poona (Pune). After his initial education at Lawrence School Sanawar, he joined the National Defence Academy and was commissioned into 17 POONA HORSE from Indian Military Academy. His regiment joined the battle in December 1971, less than six month after he joined.

2/Lt Arun Khetarpal

On the night of 16 December 1971, Indian Army after having crossed the International Border established a Bridgehead across River Basantar. Pakistani reaction was swift and fierce against the bridgehead. During the early hours of next morning, the battle situation for the Indian troops, who were in the Bridgehead, was grim. Pakistani Artillery was raining shells unceasingly and their tanks were getting into battle formation to churn and overrun the initial bridgehead. Alpha Squadron POONA HORSE was inside the Bridgehead providing support to the Infantry but it was not adequate to ward off the impending threat. Alpha Squadron Commander asked for reinforcement. Arun was commanding a troop of tanks of Bravo Squadron and was located near the Bridgehead. He heard the request for reinforcement and on orders, he moved into the Bridgehead quickly.

En-route, his Troop encountered a few enemy tanks. Both sides were surprised. However, the initiative was with Arun. He shocked the enemy by heavy volume of fire from close quarters and destroyed a few tanks. The enemy tanks withdrew and Arun proceeded further into the Bridgehead against minor opposition. At the Bridgehead, he realised that there were a large number of enemy tanks forming up from more than one direction for counter attack. During the fire fight, one of his tanks became casualty. With only two tanks left, he proceeded further un-deterred and kept on engaging the enemy tanks, which were heading towards the Bridgehead. The second tank of his Troop was also hit by enemy tank and its gun was silenced. In the ensuing close quarter fight, his own tank received a hit and the track was blown off. His commanding officer asked him to disengage and withdraw, to which he said, "No Sir, I am not abandoning my tank. My gun is still working and I will get these bastards" and went on firing with his main gun and destroyed one more enemy tank. His total tally was four tanks. Though his gun was still firing, his tank was immobile. There were just two tanks left in the bridgehead; one was a trackless Indian tank and another was a Pakistani tank.

They were well within the range of each other. Then, both tanks fired simultaneously. (The Pak tank commander, who became a Brigadier; the only living witness and the one who fired at Arun, confirmed this later.) Arun's tank received a direct hit and his tank went up in flames along with Arun.

Arun was awarded PVC for his heroic deeds beyond the call of duty. For him, it was a glorious way to die on that day and to live forever in our memory. The youngest officer of the Indian Army to have been decorated with the highest bravery award in war; regrettably it was posthumous.

He was too young to have the strategic perception of the importance of the victory in the Battle of Basantar. For him, the first credo of the Indian Military Academy given below was good enough to do what was expected of him and more.

> "THE SAFETY, HONOUR AND WELFARE OF
> YOUR COUNTRY COME FIRST, ALWAYS AND EVERY
> TIME.
>
> THE HONOUR, WELFARE AND COMFORT OF
> THE MEN YOU COMMAND COME NEXT.
>
> YOUR OWN EASE, COMFORT AND SAFETY COME LAST,
> ALWAYS AND EVERY TIME."

IN THE WORDS OF A PAKISTAN ARMY BRIGADIER

Retired Brigadier M L Khetarpal of Indian Army was born in Sargodha (now in Pakistan) in 1920. In his old age in 2001, he desired to visit his place of birth. The travel papers were prepared by his friends and they facilitated his visit to Pakistan.

At Lahore airport, his unknown host received him and took him to his home in Lahore. The visit to Sargodha and hospitality throughout his stay in Pakistan was, in the words of Brig Khetarpal, 'most memorable'. The hospitality of his host himself, all the members of his family and servants touched him. However, there was something in the eyes of every member of the family of his newly found friend, which Brig Khetarpal could not explain.

At the end of the visit, on the night before he left Lahore for New Delhi, his Host sat close to Brig Khetarpal and said, *"Sir, there is something that I wanted to tell you for many years but I did not know how to get through to you. Finally, fate has intervened and sent you to me as an honoured guest. The last few days, we have become close to one another and that has made my task even more difficult. It is regarding your son who is, of course, a national hero in India. However, on that fateful day, your son and I were soldiers, unknown to one another, fighting for the respect and safety of our respective countries. I regret to tell you that your son died in my hands. Arun's courage was exemplary and he moved his tank with fearless courage and daring, totally unconcerned about his safety. Tank casualties were very high till finally there were just two of us left facing one another. We both fired simultaneously. It was destined that I was to live and he was to die."* The Host was a retired Brigadier from Pakistan Army and the name is Khawja Mohammed Naser. Arun was the son of Brig Khetarpal.

A few days after his return home from the sentimental journey to Pakistan, Brigadier Khetarpal received an envelope containing a few photographs covering his visit to Pakistan along with a note from his host. The note read as follows:

"With Warmest regards and utmost sincerity, To: Brigadier M.L. Khetarpal, father of Shaheed Second Lieutenant Arun Khetarpal, PVC, who stood like an insurmountable rock, between the victory and failure, of the counter attack by the 'SPEARHEADS' 13 LANCERS on 16 December 1971 in the battle of "Bara Pind' as we call it and battle of "Basantar' as 17 Poona Horse remembers. Khawja Mohammad Naser, 13 Lancers, 2 March 2001, Lahore, Pakistan"

MANY FIRSTS

Major Chewang Rinchen, MVC, SM, the young hero of 1948 and 1962 war was destined to achieve greater glory. His ambition to liberate those areas of Ladakh which were annexed by Pakistan in 1948 was about to be fulfilled. He was presented with the opportunity to recapture Turtuk in 1971.

Turtuk is a large beautiful village along the Shyok River (presently it is a major tourist attraction in Ladakh) inside Baltistan. This is a Muslim dominated area of Ladakh, which was annexed by the Pak raiders in 1948 and remained with Pakistan. Being located between the Northern Areas of POK and Aksai Chin/Karakoram frontier, this area is strategically important for the defense of Ladakh. Pakistan could use this area as a launching pad for attack into Ladakh. Turtuk Sector also controls over the vital Thoise Airbase in Ladakh.

During the 1971 Indo-Pak war, having gained an overall upper hand in the war, it was considered strategically beneficial if India could recapture areas bordering Partapur and Kargil. Approximately three Company of Karakoram Scouts were guarding these areas. Some of the Pakistani posts in this area were located at the height of 18000 feet and above.

Major Chewang Rinchen, MVC, SM with three Company of Ladakh Scouts and four Company of Nubra Guards trained by him lead the advance. This operation known as 'Battles on Top of the World' started on 8 December. The unsurpassed high altitude warriors of Ladakh, unmindful of the adverse weather conditions and extremely rugged high altitude terrain, advanced 22 kms into the enemy territory in just 14 days and captured Chalunka and Turtuk along with five more villages and Pt 18402; the highest post ever captured by any Army the world over. (The exception being the capture of Bana Post in Siachen in a special op much later) The bold actions and personal exemplary leadership of Major Rinchen lead to series of tactical victory and inspired his men to excel beyond human comprehension.

The cease-fire which was declared on 16 December 1971 was heaven sent to the demoralised Pakistanis. Had the war continued for a few more days, Rinchen and his brave men would have continued their advance deeper into Baltistan region and would have completed the task that was left undone in 1948. (This also would have prevented the ongoing Siachen problems)

They liberated 804 sq kms of territory which was legitimately Indian. This is more than the total territorial gain made in 1965 war. All this was achieved with just three of our men wounded in action. The enemy suffered 19 dead and many more wounded. A total of 36 POW were taken.

Major Rinchen was awarded Bar to Maha Vir Chakra for his bold actions, personal bravery and inspiring leadership. This was the Second Maha Vir Chakra awarded to him. Thus he became the:

- First Ladakhi to be enrolled as National Guard at the age of 17.
- First to be promoted as Jemadar at the age of 17.
- First to be honored with Maha Vir Chakra at the age of 17.
- First to be awarded MVC and Sena Medal.
- First and only Ladakhi to be awarded with two MVCs (MVC Bar).
- First Ladakhi to be promoted to the Rank of Colonel.
- First Ladakhi Hony Colonel of an Infantry Regiment.

Major Chewang Rinchen, MVC, SM Receiving MVC Bar

He retired from the Army in the Rank of Colonel. Many of the Army and Civil Institutions have been named after this unique and brave officer who went to achieve Many Firsts. (Regrettably he is no more)

A STRING OF BARBED WIRE

Major Kuldip Singh Chandpuri took a bold decision to stay put at Longewala Border Post when it was under intense threat from numerically superior mechanised units of Pakistan Army. It was a momentous decision. He and his 120 men of Alfa Company 23 PUNJAB took over this erstwhile Border Security Force Post just a few days before Pakistani Air Force launched pre-emptive strikes on the forward air bases of India on 3 December 1971.

Major K S Chandpuri

Since the creation of East and West Pakistan, their military leaders had opted for Ayub Khan's doctrine that 'defence of East Pakistan lies in the West'. Accordingly, in 1971, after the Bengali Muslims with the help of India, attacked the well entrenched Pak Army in East Pakistan, Yahya Khan their President, ordered his Army to launch an offensive in the West with a view to draw out the Indian Forces from the east which will reduce pressure on the Pak Army there.

Pakistani Generals planned an offensive operation to capture a vast Indian desert territory up to Jaisalmer in Rajasthan. Their outline plan was to advance upto Longewala on a broad front and capture it by D plus 1. From there, further advance towards Ramgarh using the Border Roads and then on to Jaisalmer. Their plan was lauded in the words one of their brigadiers, Tariq Mir as; *"Insha Allah (God willing) we will have breakfast at Longewala, lunch at Ramgarh and dinner at Jaisalmer"*.

He probably would have had his meals as desired if they had captured Longewala. From there, well connected Border Roads would have made their task easier. There were hardly any Indian Army units between Longewala and Jaisalmer. All this dream of having dinner at Jaisalmer was

A String of Barbed Wire

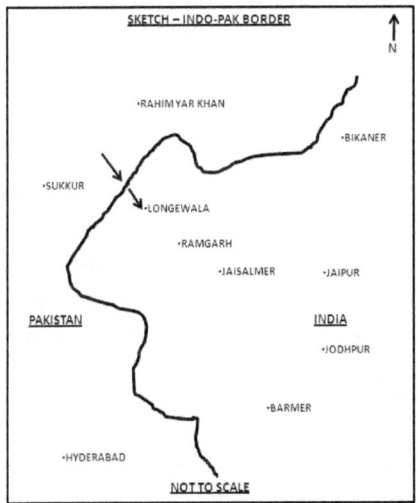

thwarted by Chandpuri and the brave men of Alfa Company 23 PUNJAB who were defending Longewala; *the only military post en-route to Ramgarh*. Indian Air Force (Forward Air base) located at Jaisalmer played a crucial role.

Longewala was an isolated post without any mutual support from outside or any defensive minefield. Defense works had not been completed fully to withstand a large-scale attack at Longewala. There was no time to lay even protective minefields. The Company had just one anti-tank weapon capable of firing beyond 500m. It had some artillery support from outside.

Immediately after the Pakistani pre-emptive air strike on the Indian forward air bases on 3 December 1971, Major Chandpuri decided to throw the eyes and ears of his Post and had sent a party of 20 men under Lieutenant Dharamvir from Longewala to the International Border to observe enemy movement.

On the night 4/5 December 1971, Dharamvir reported that Pakistani Forces *comprising of infantry and tanks* crossed the International Border and were heading towards Longewala. Further he said, that the tanks were carrying infantrymen on the top. He was asked to shadow the Pakistani Forces and provide continuous information on their further movement.

Major Chandpuri passed on his assessment of an impending Pakistani attack on his Post to his Commanding Officer. Having realized the gravity of the situation, his Commanding Officer gave him the option to withdraw from Longewala to the Battalion Headquarter location, which was about 16 Kms away.

It was a major dilemma. He neither had time to organise an orderly withdrawal nor was he willing to concede the territory up to Ramgarh without a fight. Any attempt to carry out a tactical withdrawal would have ended in a Waterloo. Therefore, he decided to stay there against all odds and give a good fight from his defences rather than opting for sure destruction of his command dishonourably in the hands of enemy while withdrawing to a rear location. The poor state of defence preparedness notwithstanding, Chandpuri and his men resolved to fight until the last man and last round. It was to be a fight of 120 versus 2,500; a defining moment in the history.

Just before the enemy shelling commenced, Chandpuri ordered his men to lay a few mines on the likely approaches of enemy tanks. Sepoy Bishan Das with his Pioneer section quickly laid a few scattered mine fields and closed the gap in the three strands of barbed wire fence which was laid earlier to prevent animals, especially stray camels, from entering into the post. Major Chandpuri went around his defences, readjusted the location of the anti-tank weapons to cover the most likely enemy tank approach to his Post. He visited all the bunkers and spoke to his brave men emphasizing the need for strict fire discipline. Shoot only to kill

At about 3 AM, the Post was under heavy artillery fire. When the Pakistani Tanks closed in with the Post, the accurate fire of the anti-tank weapons from the Post destroyed two of them. One more tank had its track blown off probably due to mine. Thereafter, Pak tanks did not come closer to the Post. They encircled the Post from all directions but did not cross the barbed wire fence. The enemy tanks were carrying barrels filled with diesel on top of the tanks as reserve. Some of these barrels exploded in the shelling and lit up the entire area. This aided the defenders to take accurate aim on the enemy tanks and vehicles. By about 5 AM, Pak had lost 12 tanks and a large number of other vehicles.

Around 6 AM, an Indian Army Forward Air Controller pilot, Major Atma Singh, flew over the battle area in his small plane and reported of a large concentration of enemy including tanks between the International Border and Longewala. Then help came from the heavens. Indian Air Force Hunter aircrafts from Jaiselmer Forward Air Base took off by first light (these fighters did not have night vision devices in those days) and destroyed many tanks and vehicles stranded in the open. The whole of next day, there was no

Pakistani air cover to oppose Indian Air Force. Indian Fighter Aircrafts had a field day and destroyed as many as 26 tanks and hundreds of other Armed Personnel Carriers and light vehicles.

A Pakistani attempt to bypass Longewala and advance towards Ramgarh proved to be costly in terms of tank causality. The momentum of Pak attack petered out. Thus, the ill-prepared and over- ambitious military adventure of Pakistan ended in a debacle. One of the Pakistani commanders while requesting for air support on radio set said, *"The enemy air force has been creating havoc - One aircraft leaves and another comes and stays overhead for twenty minutes. 40% troops and tanks have been destroyed, injured or damaged. Further advance has become very difficult. Send air force for help as soon as possible otherwise even a safe withdrawal would be difficult."* Indeed, it did become difficult even to withdraw to their safety due to the relentless air attacks by our Air Force pilots.

One wonders why Pakistani Army particularly the tanks, did not assault Longewala defences. As John F Kennedy said, "Victory has many fathers, but defeat is an orphan." Conjectures are many. Some say Pakistani Generals did not plan properly and had no air support what so ever allotted to this operation. One more reason stated was that the leading elements of the attacker were surprised by the accuracy and intensity of fire brought down on them from Longewala Post. This led them to over-estimate the strength of the Post including minefields. Three innocuous strings of barbed wires were mistaken for the minefield markings, thus the tanks did not assault. Yet another belief is that Tanot Mata (Ma Durga) saved India. (The beautiful temple at Tanot is maintained by the BSF. Pakistani Air Force during 1965 and 1971 war dropped many bombs here, but none of them has ever exploded)

The bold decision taken by Major Kuldip Singh Chandpuri to stay put and fight, the bravery and resoluteness of his men and the good shooting of our pilots had averted a major defeat and loss of a large chunk of the Indian Territory. Had Pakistan Army captured Longewala and reached our Border Roads, there was nothing else after that to prevent them from having their dinner at Jaisalmer.

Major Chandpuri (later Brigadier) was awarded Maha Vir Chkra. Ten Vir Chakras were awarded to others. The Pakistani General responsible for the operation was dismissed from service.

The military historians have recorded that in this battle, the proportion of causality suffered by tanks and infantry was the highest after the World War II. Pakistan had lost more than 200 men, 36 tanks and large number of other vehicles; whereas, Indian Army loss was two men, an anti-tank gun and a few camels.

Thus ended 1971 war with decisive victory to India both in the east and west and birth of a new nation; Bangladesh. India had a limited aim of finding solution to the refugee problems created by East Pakistan in 1971. However, it was Pakistan which opened a second Front in the west by attacking the Indian air bases on 3 December 1971. While taking the initiative in the east, India had visualized the need to maintain balance at all time. Therefore, the Indian Forces met the challenges of Pak attack in Jammu, Punjab and Rajasthan Sector. Both Armies used their mechanised forces to undertake offensive operations. Indian Army primarily used their tanks in anti-tank role and destroyed large number of Pakistani tanks.

For the first time, our special forces conducted raids deep inside the Pakistani territory behind the enemy lines successfully during this war. Raid on a gun position at Mandhol across Poonch River during 1971 War by the 9 Para Commando resulted in the destruction of guns, ammunition and other vital equipment. Pakistanis suffered 37 killed, 41 wounded. The unit was awarded the Battle Honour, 'Defence of Poonch' in the 1971 war. In Rajasthan 10 Para Commando conducted many raids in Chachro and Islamgarh.

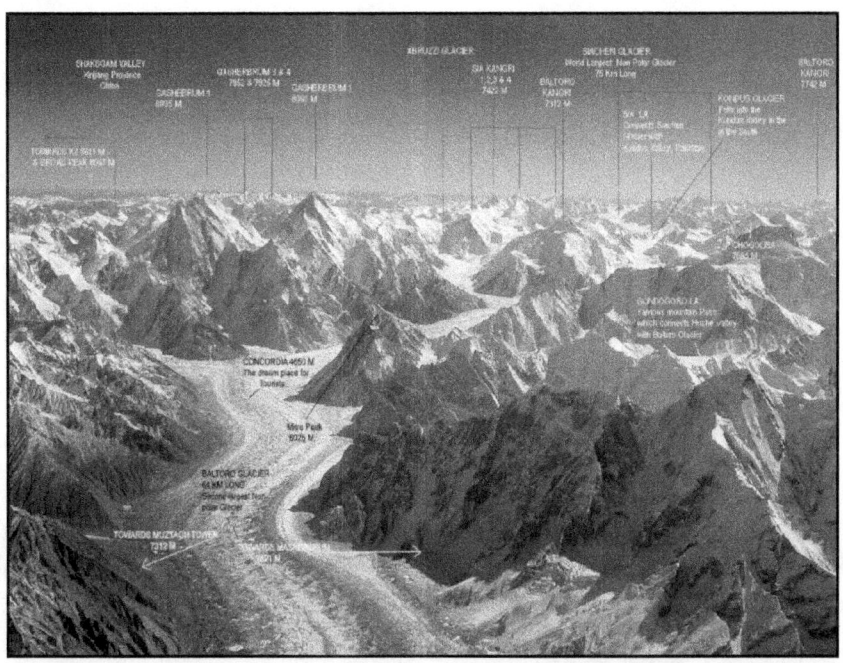

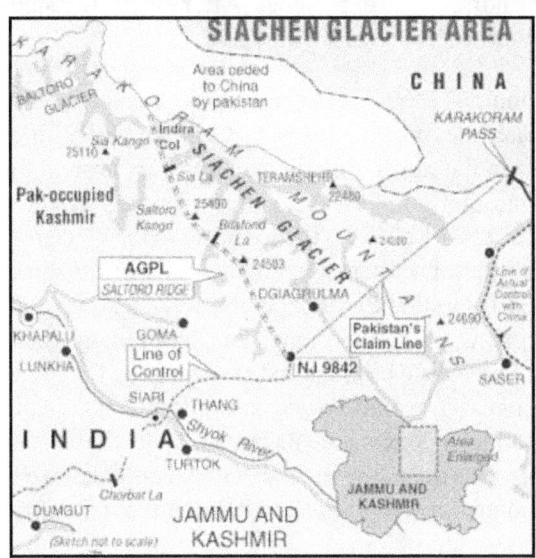

SIACHEN JUST IN TIME

*We secured Siachen at a great cost. If we ever vacate Saltoro Ridge,
we will never be able to recapture it.*

-Hony Capt Bana Singh PVC.

Tom Long staff gave the name Siachen. It means 'the area of black (wild) roses'. This 70 odd kms long Siachen Glacier is located on the eastern Karakoram Ranges. To its west is the Saltoro Ridge line and to the east is Karakoram Ranges. The Saltoro Ridge originates from the Sia kangri Peak located on the Chinese border. The altitude of the Ridge Line varies from 17,880 to 25,300 feet. There are three major passes on this Ridge namely, Sia La, (18,336 feet) Bilafond La (17,880 feet) and Gyong La (18,665 feet).

The average annual snowfall in this area is about 35 feet and temperature goes down to minus 50 degree Centigrade. Normal human habitations cannot survive in this area. Rarified air above 9000 feet leads to breathing problems. Pulmonary oedema, cold injuries, such as frostbite, chilblains and hypoxia are the most common disease. Shaving and answering to nature's call are horrendous experience. After every fifty steps or so one has to rest a while before he can walk further.

The Line of Control (LOC) / Cease Fire Line (CFL) between POK and India is not demarcated beyond the point at Grid Ref NJ 98200420 up to the Chinese border in the north. The dispute revolves around the extension of the LOC beyond this point on the Saltoro Range. Karachi agreement of 1949 states, (from NJ 9820420) "thence north to the glaciers". There was no mention of it in the subsequent agreements. Therefore, our claim has been that the LOC/CFL should be extended northwards along the Saltoro Range up to Sia Kangri. On the other hand, Pakistan's stand is, that beyond NJ 9820420, the LOC should be extended eastwards up to the Karakoram pass. Neither the word east nor Karakoram pass is found in the said Agreement to claim the direction of extension of the LOC to the east. If the LOC is extended northwards the entire Siachen Glacier and Saltoro Ridge area will form part of Indian Territory, whereas if extended it to east, it would go to Pakistan.

In the 1970s and early 1980s, Pakistan had been permitting several mountaineering expeditions to other countries to climb high peaks on this glacier unilaterally; thus indirectly claiming the ownership of this area. Since 1978, the Indian Army began closely monitoring the situation and subsequently allowed mountaineering expeditions to the glacier from our side. The most notable was the one in which Colonel N Kumar led an Army expedition to Teram Kangri Peaks.

Col N Kumar PVSM, KC, AVSM, FRGS

In the early eighties, based on a reliable intelligence input, India realized that Pak had the ulterior motive of annexing the Siachen Glacier in the near future and was preparing for it. To thwart such an initiative, India launched 'Operation Maghdoot'. This was to secure the Passes on the Saltoro Ridge and other tactically important features in the Glacier. 4 Kumaon was tasked to secure the Passes on the Saltaro Ridge. The Battalion along with the troops of Ladak Scout planned this operation using the advise/information, maps/sketches and films provided by the legendary mountaineer, Colonel Narendra Kumar PVSM, KC, AVSM, FRGS. On 13 April 1984, an airborne operation was launched. They landed and occupied the Bilafond La Pass. Four days later, another force occupied the Sia La pass on the same Ridge. Major RS Sandhu, Captain Sanjay Kulkarni and Captain PV Yadav had led these operations.

Siachen Valley

Having realized that the game was over even before it began for them, Pakistan Army on April 24/25, attempted to dislodge our troops from the Bilafond La, but failed in their attempt. In the days that followed, the Indian Army had built up a large force to defend the Saltoro Ridgeline. Since then, the Saltoro Range has been the focal point of operations; the Pakistanis seeking to gain a foothold on the Ridge line, the Indians denying it.

In the early April 1987, a small force consisting of Pakistani SSG commandos, using ropes and ladders, climbed up a vertical cliff and occupied a small plateau at 22,143ft. They named it as Quaid Post. This Post, the highest military post established any where in the world, dominates our positions at Bilafond La. Although the Passes and the heights dominating them were in our control, Quaid Post effectively dominated the approach to those heights.

Our Posts are air maintained. (Most of the Pakistani Posts are maintained by road or by mule train). Anyone who controls Quaid Post can control the air operations on the Saltoro Ridge and interfere with our life line; the helicopter operations. Therefore, many attempts were made to evict the Pak forces from Quaid Post unsuccessfully. With Quaid Post in the hands of Pakistan Army, it was becoming increasingly difficult to maintain our Forces on the Ridgeline. Therefore, in May 87, it was decided to launch a deliberate attack to capture Quaid Post by 8 J&K LI, commanded by Col AP Rai. Quaid Post was estimated to be held by a section of Pak SSG men, commanded by Subedar Ataullah Mohammed.

On 29 May, a patrol under Lt Rajiv Pande was sent to identify a safe approach route to Quaid Post and mark it with guide ropes. Rajiv did succeed in his task but he and eight of his men made their ultimate sacrifice during this operation. Those who returned to the Base confirmed that the guide ropes had been fixed.

The attack was planned for 23 June 1987. The attacking team comprised of two officers, three JCOs and 58 men of 8 J&K LI. The operation was code named as OP RAJIV in honor of late Lt Pande. The Commander was Major Virendar Singh. This attack involved a steep vertical climb of over 1500 ft and then an assault. Attcking team was assembled one by one over 20 days.

On 23 June, the first assault was launched to capture the Post under Virender. However, it did not succeed, as the guide rope fixed by late Lt Pande could not be found. Again, on 25th second attempt was made under

Subedar Harnam Singh. They found the rope but due to enemy interference and lack of communication, the assault did not succeed. They came under enemy fire and were forced to spend the day in the open. They were tired and running out of food. Finally, on 26th June, Virendar decided to launch a day light attack from two directions. The two teams were lead by Virender and N/Sub Bana Singh.

The team under Bana Singh comprised of Riflemen Chunni Lal, Laxman Das, Om Raj and Kashmir Chand. They selected a longer and difficult approach from an unexpected direction to the Post. They crawled up and crept close to the top. Using the cover provided by blizzard and very poor visibility, they approached the lone bunker on top from behind. Having realized that their rifle had suffered cold arrest, Bana pulled out a grenade, lobbed it into the bunker and closed the door. The explosion within the confined space of the bunker was devastating. When later the bunker door was opened, they found that all those who were inside the bunker were dead. Others who were outside the bunker were bayoneted and killed. Those who tried to escape fell into the abyss. Later a total of six dead bodies were recovered and handed over to Pak Army.

N/Sub Bana Singh PVC

Virendar was severely wounded by an artillery shell after the Post was captured. They were tired and hungry. They had no energy left to celebrate their achievement. Message of congratulations were pouring in. Bana Singh was told that henceforth, Pak Quaid Post would be called Bana Top. The impact of his achievement was enormous.

Naib Subedar Bana Singh was awarded Param Vir Chakra for the most conspicuous gallantry and inspiring leadership under adverse conditions. A Maha Vir Chakra was awarded to Subedar Harnam Singh and 7 Vir Chakras including one each to Major Virendar Singh, Lieutenant Pande and Rifleman Om Raj were also awarded for bravery. This feat of valor of the 8

J&K L I is etched in the annals of High Altitude Warfare as one without parallels. *"Quartered in snow, silent to remain When the bugle calls, they shall rise and march again.*

Naib Subedar later Subedar Major Hony Capt Bana Singh was born in 1949 in J&K and joined the J&K LI. In keeping with the tradition, his son has also joined the same Regiment.

Post Script:

Having lost their Quaid Post and in turn, their ambition to establish a foothold on the Saltoro Ridge militarily, Pak is trying to negotiate it politically. As many as eight meetings had been held without achieving any result. Pakistan's refusal to authenticate their present ground holding positions is a clear indication of her ambition to grab this land. Will India ever succumb to the demands of these unreliable land grabbers?

THE FOURTH ATTEMPT AT KARGIL

It was our own fault, and our very grave fault, and now we must turn it to use.

-Kipling

In spite of the three-failed attempt to annex Kargil since 1947, a fourth attempt was made to capture Kargil in 1999 by Pakistan. To make such frequent and desperate attempt, to take so much of trouble and suffer repeated loss of face; Kargil must be very important for Pakistan. For India, it is very important to retain and control Kargil District for more than one vital reason. The lifeline; the Road Srinagar- Leh, passes through Kargil Town. The alignment of this Road; both towards east and west of Kargil for over 100 kms, is nearly parallel to the Line Of Control (LOC) and passes within the effective range of Pak Army long range artillery weapons deployed along the LOC. In spite of the alternative route now available to connect Leh via Rohtang Pass, Srinagar-Leh Road has remained the life line for the entire Ladakh. Batalik Sub-Sector located east of Kargil provides depth and access to Siachen. Therefore, Kargil has remained a vital area for the security of Ladakh.

Having come out only the second best in their attempt to annex Siachen in 1984, Pakistan wanted to avenge the Siachen fiasco in Kargil and was waiting for an opportunity. The unwritten Gentleman's Agreement provided the long awaited opportunity to Pakistan in 1999. Some border posts in the higher reaches of Kargil used to be vacated during the peak winter months from October to March by both sides. During the winter months of 1998/99, as usual, our non-maintainable Posts were vacated. Pakistan Army units, particularly, Northern Light Infantry units along with local militants, not only did not vacate their posts but they entered into the Indian side of the LOC and occupied some of the dominating Posts on our side of the LOC at Mushkoh, Dras, Kaksar, Batalik, Turtok and the Haneef sub-sectors. Having occupied the vacant posts, they strengthened the defense works by March 1999 with mine field and additional bunkers.

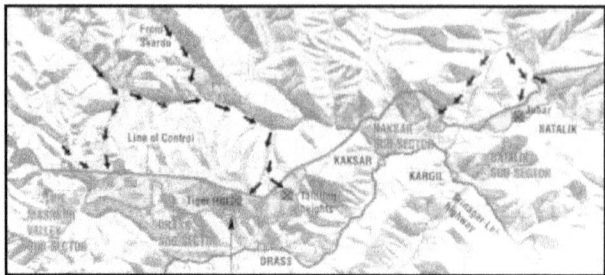

Kargil Sector

During May 1999, the locals warned Indian Army units holding the LOC that Pakistan may have violated the unwritten Gentleman's Agreement which was in vogue from 1987. This was confirmed when a patrol lead by Capt Kalia did not return. (The members of the patrol were captured and killed by Pakistanis after torturing them.) Later, all the units deployed in Kargil Sector confirmed the presence of Pakistani troops inside Indian Territory. Action taken by the local units to evict Pakistanis did not produce any result. It was later estimated that about 5000 Pakistanis had intruded into Indian side of the LOC and were in occupation of roughly 200 sq kms of our territory from the Dras Sub-Sector in the west to Batalik in the east.

Having realized the gravity of the situation, Indian Army planned a counter offensive to evict the intruders from the Indian side of LOC. Large number of Infantry and Artillery units were rushed to Kargil Sector. Weather God and the Border Road Task Force facilitated the large-scale induction of units by early opening of Zojila Pass. The counter offensive was code named as Operation Vijay which commenced on 06 June 99 and lasted till July 27.

In high altitude mountainous terrain, the attack is launched with sections and platoons sequentially (in echelon/ waves) one behind the other due to restricted availability of frontage for a large scale attack. The ratio of troops required of the attackers as against the defenders is very high. As the saying goes, mountain eats up the troops; especially the attacking troops. In Kargil

Dras Valley

Tololing

war, for every Infantry soldier who attacked the enemy bunker, ten men were employed to provide support to him.

Important objectives that were required to be recaptured in order to reopen the Srinagar Leh Road were, Tiger Hill and Tololing in Dras Sub-Sector and Jubar Hills in Batalic Sub-Sector. Tiger Hill complex could only be approached after clearing Tololing. Therefore, Tololing which was held by the intruders in strength had to be recaptured first. Tough battles were fought for every bunker held by the enemy in these areas by our Infantry units duly supported by excellent and innovative artillery fire support.

18 Grenadiers, 1 Naga, and 8 Sikh, 13 JAK RIF and 2 RAJ RIF were involved in the recapture of Dras Sector. 18 Grenadiers commanded by Col Kushal Thakur was tasked to recapture a part of Tololing. The representation made by the Commanding Officer to delay the attack by a few days for thorough preparation and request for additional fire power were not considered favourably by higher headquarters. He launched the attack as directed. The battle for Tololing began on the 20 May 1999. The attack was planned from three sides to capture the Tololing Top, Area Flat and Point 4590. The enemy who was well entrenched at those tops, was able to observe the attackers movement and bring down effective aimed fire on them.

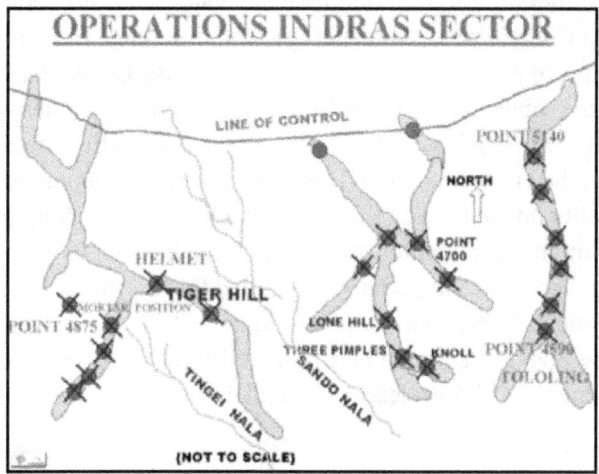

Two assaults were launched by 18 Grenadiers, but they were repulsed. B Company led by Major Rajesh Adhikari launched the third assault. Adhikari and his men succeeded in reaching very close to the enemy bunkers. Then, the numerically superior enemy surrounded them. A fierce close combat took place in which Adhikari along with Subedar Randhir Singh, Lance Naik R K Yadav and Grenadier Parveen Kumar were killed. The rest withdrew. Most of them were either wounded or sick from high altitude effects. Major Adhikari was awarded MVC for his bravery of exceptional order. 18 Grenadiers were asked to come back to their firm base.

Another attack under the second in command of the Battalion, Lt Col Vishwanathan was launched. After six hours of climb, Viswanathan launched the attack. However, the attack did not succeed against well coordinated fire of the enemy. Repeated failure forced the higher commanders to realise that their attack did not have hard enough punch to destroy the enemy with their existing resources. They had to seek and obtain additional fire power. Subsequently, about 250 artillery guns including Bofors were brought in to clear the infiltrators from Kargil Sector. In spite of restricted deployment space, Bofors FH-77B field howitzer played a vital role. They were very effective in direct firing role even with a single gun.

13 JAK Rifles commanded by Lt Colonel YK Joshi was tasked to capture the Area up to Knoll and clear Point 5140. The Unit moved directly from Sopore in Kashmir Valley to the base of Tololing. A day attack was launched on 17 June. Area up to Knoll was captured after fierce hand-to-hand fighting. Captain Vikram Batra, who had recently returned from Commando Course, was commanding Delta Company. His Company was given the task of recapturing Point 5140. This brave Officer had decided to approach the objective from behind and cut off the enemy route of withdrawal. He and his men climbed the near vertical rock-cliff and approached the enemy location. However, the enemy taking advantage of good visibility opened heavy fire at the attackers. Batra, along with five of his men, climbed up and after reaching the top, hurled two grenades at the machine gun post. He single-handedly killed three enemy soldiers in close combat. Though he was injured, he reorganized his group, charged at the next enemy position and captured Point 5140 at 0330 hours on 20 June 1999. The enemy withdrew leaving behind their machine gun.

Captain Vikram Batra

Capt Batra along with Capt Anuj Nayyar had led his men to further victory with the recapture of Point 4750 and Point 4875. Batra was killed while fighting at Point 4875 on 7 July 1999. Captain Vikram Batra had fought with exceptional courage and tenacity against all odds. For his display of the most conspicuous personal bravery in the face of the enemy, Captain Vikram Batra was awarded Param Vir Chakra. In recognition of his gallant act, Point 4875 has been renamed as Captain Vikram Batra Top.

Another important objective to be recaptured by 13 JAK RIF was Flat Top in Mushkoh Valley. Major Gurpreet's Company was tasked to capture the Flat Top. The leading Scout was Rifleman Sanjay Kumar. The advance on the face of the enemy was difficult and slow. The enemy was well entrenched and had good domination of the area.

Rfn Sanjay Kumar

Having scaled the cliff, the Company met with very heavy enemy fire. Sanjay was about 150 meters away from the first enemy bunker. With complete disregard to his personal safety, Sanjay crawled up to the bunker and charged. Though he was hit in his chest, he continued to charge and silenced the nearest bunker. Then he picked-up an enemy machine-gun and attacked the next enemy bunker. He killed three enemies on the spot. Inspired by his brave act, the rest of his team followed him and captured other bunkers. Taken by surprise, the enemy fled leaving behind their weapons and equipment.

For his display of the most conspicuous personal bravery and gallantry of the highest order in the face of the enemy, Rifleman Sanjay Kumar was awarded Nation's highest wartime gallantry award; PVC. In the whole of this operation, all ranks had exhibited a high standard of professionalism and motivation. The Battalion was awarded the Battle Honor and two PVC and eight VrC.

1 NAGA Battalion captured Black Rock, Thumps Up, Pyramid (all part of Point 5140), Pimple Hill (later renamed as Naga Hill) and Point 5060. The battalion was awarded with two Vir Chakra and two Sena Medals for their outstanding performance during this operation.

2 Raj Rif was inducted into the Kargil Battle from Kupwara during the ongoing offensive to capture Tololing. A few previous attempts made by the other units had not succeeded in capturing Tololing completely. 2 Raj Rif after a thorough preparation, including a mock attack on a similar feature, launched their attack. Their first assault was held up. The second assault lead by Capt Vijyant however captured their objective successfully on the early morning of 13 June 1999. The recapture of Tololing was the turning point of the war.

2 Raj Rif continued their winning spree from Tololing onwards. Their next task was to capture Three Pimples and Knoll. Here the enemy had improved the defenses and their position was well stocked for a prolonged battle. The attack commenced with a fierce artillery barrage. Capt Vijyant's platoon was in the lead. The enemy responded with an equally intense and accurate bombardment on the attacking troops. However, the indomitable men of A Company managed to establish a foothold on the objective. After two hours of fierce fighting, Knoll was captured. During the close combat, Major P Acharya was killed. This shocked the brave Vijyant and the men of his Company. They charged a lone machine gun bunker from where the fire was causing heavy casualty and silenced it before a burst of fire killed Vijyant. He fell dead in the arms of his comrade NK Tilak Singh. Once the machine gun bunker was neutralized, the rest of the Company advanced and captured their objective. In this operation, the Battalion had lost three officers and

The Fourth Attempt at Kargil

Tiger Hill

three more were severely injured. 10 OR were killed and 42 wounded. The Battalion was awarded four MVCs and six VrCs for bravery.

18 Grenadiers was once again tasked to capture; this time, the Tiger Hill. Tiger Hill is 5062m high and has sharp conical features. It stands a few km north of Dras. Tiger hill extends about 2200 meters from west to east and 1000m from north to south. There is a large extension towards the west on which there are two spurs. The first one approximately 500m west of Tiger Hill is known as *India Gate,* and the second, another 300m to the west is called *Helmet*. It was estimated to be held with approximately one company of the enemy.

Gren YS Yadav

18 Grenadiers, 2 Naga and 8 Sikh were preparing for the final assault on Tiger Hill. They were supported with artillery, engineer and adequate logistic support. Around 200 men were involved in the assault while 2000 men provided support. The Air Force engaged Tiger Hill and had several bulls' eyes on it. 18 Grenadiers was to launch the attack from the East with 8 Sikh providing firm base for the attack. 8 Sikh was also tasked to simulate attacks from the South and North and to cut off Tiger Hill from the West. This would effectively isolate Tiger Hill.

At 0130 hrs on 4 July 99, 18 Grenadiers launched an attack and managed to establish a foot hold. The Grenadiers kept up their relentless pressure on the enemy and in spite of inclement weather and numerous counter attacks at every stage of attack, they progressed their attack capturing enemy held bunkers, one after the other. Lt Balwan Singh led the commando platoon of 18 Granadiers on the most difficult northeastern approach. His team consisted of 18 men. Grenadier Yogender Singh Yadav was part of the Commando Platoon.

The approach was a near vertical cliff face with snow-covered at 16,500 feet. Grenadier Yogender Singh Yadav, volunteering to lead the assault, was climbing the cliff face and fixing the ropes for further assault on the feature. Halfway up, an enemy bunker opened up machine gun and rocket fire. His Platoon Commander Lt Balwan Singh and two others fell back against the heavy volume of automatic fire.

Realising the enormity of the situation, Yadav continued to scale the cliff face alone through a volley of fire. In spite of having been hit by three bullets in his groin and shoulder, displaying superhuman strength and resolve, he climbed the remaining 60 feet, all by himself and reached the top. With rare grit and courage, he crawled up to the bunker and lobbed a grenade killing four Pakistani soldiers and neutralising enemy fire. This act was directly instrumental in facilitating the rest of the platoon in climbing up the cliff face.

Grievously injured, but with total disregard to personal safety, Grenadier Yogender Singh Yadav with two of his colleagues charged on to the second bunker and neutralised it after a fierce hand-to-hand combat; killing three Pakistani soldiers. This extraordinarily gallant act facilitated the rest of the platoon, which quickly traversed the treacherous terrain and braving hostile fire, charged onto the enemy to capture Tiger Hill, a vital objective.

For this display of indomitable spirit, determination and action beyond the call of duty and sustained display of the most conspicuous personal bravery and gallantry of the highest order in the face of the enemy, he was decorated with Param Vir Chakra.

Area Pt 4875 is located west of Tiger Hill. It is a strategically important feature northwest of Dras and dominating National Highway 1A. From this feature, one can also observe all movement into the Mushkoh valley from the East. The recapture of Pt 4875 was an operational imperative to evict the enemy from the Mushkoh valley. 13 JAK RIF, with some additional resources in support, recaptured this by 05 July 1999 after a decisive fight.

Lt K Clifford Nongrum

Lt K Clifford Nongrum led the commando attack on the Top of Pt 4875 and established a firm base before the main attack was launched. He was awarded MVC for his bravery and the ultimate sacrifice he made during the successful commando operation.

In the Batalik Sector the enemy had captured a vast area and posed a threat to Kargil - Leh Road. While the recapturing of important Posts were in progress in the west in Dras Sub-Sector, as many as 11 Infantry Battalions including 5 PARA,10 PARA,22 Grenadiers,17 Garhwal Rifles,1/11 GR,12 J&K LI, 1 Bihar, 14 Sikh and troops of Ladak Scout were inducted to evict the intruders from the Batalik Sub Sector. 15 Field Regiment provided artillery support. These operations took place simultaneously in some of the most treacherous terrain in the high altitude. In Batalik, Pakistanis had intruded 8-10 km across the LOC and occupied four ridge lines; Jubar, Kukarthang, Khalubar and Point 5203 at heights of 15,000-16,800 feet. The strength of the enemy in this sector was assessed to be between 600 and 800 intruders.

The operations were conducted over a period of nearly two months. Before the attack commenced, enemy logistic support was disrupted and the enemy defenses were divided into two halves. Chorbatla in the east was tackled first.

1/11 GR commanded by Col Lalit Roy, was tasked to capture Juber Top. Capt Manoj Pandey was with the leading Company. When the leading elements of his Company reached the base of the Hill Top, they came under heavy fire. Undeterred by the fire, Manoj led his men along a narrow ridge that led to the enemy position. While still short of the objective, the enemy fired upon him. Displaying great courage, he surged ahead of his troops and charged at the enemy through a hail of enemy bullets and destroyed the bunker. This in turn lead to the capture of other enemy bunkers and ultimately, the Juber Top.

After the capture of Juber, on the night of 2/3 July 1999 the Battalion launched another attack to capture Khalubar. Manoj and his men were leading the advance. They came under heavy and intense enemy fire from the surrounding heights. Manoj was tasked to clear the interfering enemy positions. He quickly moved his platoon to an advantageous position under intense enemy fire, sent one section to clear the enemy positions from the right and he himself proceeded to clear the enemy positions from the left.

Capt Manoj Pandey

Fearlessly assaulting the first enemy position, he killed two enemy personnel and destroyed the second position by killing two more. He was injured on the shoulder and legs while clearing the third bunker. Undaunted and without caring for his grievous injuries, he continued to lead the assault on the fourth and a larger bunker, urging his men to follow him and destroyed the same with a grenade. Enemy was very active and targeted Manoj with automatic weapons and grenade. A grenade exploded on his face and he was severely bleeding of his injury. Knowing full well that he will soon meet his creator, he urged his men to continue the fight and capture the objective before he died. His men fulfilled his last command.

This singular daredevil act of Manoj provided the critical firm base for the companies, which finally led to capture of Khalubar. Capt Manoj Kumar Pandey, thus, displayed most conspicuous bravery, indomitable courage, outstanding leadership and devotion to duty and made the supreme sacrifice in the highest traditions of the Indian Army. He was awarded PVC for the bravery and leadership of exceptional order in the face of the enemy and sacrifice of his life for the country.

One PVC, two MVCs and 24 VrCs were awarded in this sector for bravery. Six Battalions had earned the Battle Honour. 125 of our brave soldiers laid down their life. More tham 300 were wounded during the war.

In the entire Kargil Operations, more than five brigades of Infantry and nearly twenty regiments of artillery were employed to evict the intruders. A total of four PVCs, eight MVCs and 51 VrCs were awarded for bravery.

Thus the threat to the National Highway in kargil District and to Siachen was eliminated. In the face of severe criticism from the International community and the UNO, Pakistan withdrew the intruders from the other localities of Kargil Sector by 26 July 1999. The fourth attempt to annex Kargil by Pakistan ended in yet another fiasco for them.

A BRAVE HEART

Col NJ Nair AC, KC

NJ was a product of Sainik School Kazhakootam, Kerala and National Defense Academy, Pune. He was commissioned into 16th Battalion, the Maratha Light Infantry (MLI) in June 1971 after pre-commission training at the Indian Military Academy, Dehradun.

16 MLI was a highly motivated and well-trained unit where NJ made a name for himself. One of his Commanding Officers said, 'Men love NJ more than me.' The feeling was mutual. NJ once said, 'My Battalion was a dream place to grow up.'

NJ held many important appointments in the Battalion. Later, he was posted to the faculty in the Army Intelligence School; a tough and prestigious assignment. About his work there, he said, 'I do not know how good I was in teaching, but I do know that I learnt more while teaching there'. That is typical of NJ; a modest soldier. Later, he was selected to attend the Defense Services Staff College Course in Wellington. He graduated with excellence. NJ was an intelligent, unassuming and cheerful Maratha Officer who was always up to doing something extraordinary. As a young officer he had travelled far and wide; most of the time on his motorcycle. He was a skilled boatman and an excellent swimmer; skills that he derived from his place of birth - Ernakulum, Kerala.

During the early 80's, 16 MLI was deployed in Mizoram in counter insurgency operations against Mizo Insurgents. NJ was commanding a Company in an area that was vast, mountainous and inhospitable. This area has a navigable river, which is the lifeline for the locals. Boats and country crafts were used to carry goods and transport people. NJ came to know that insurgents were using the boats to carry goods without paying freight charges and were collecting 'taxes' forcibly from boat owners and passengers.

NJ decided to deny the use of boats to the insurgents and prevent them from collecting taxes. He made a plan and explained it to his men in detail.

Accordingly, on 13 February 1983, he hired a boat without the crew. He and one more man of his Company were disguised as local boatmen. They took the boat and headed towards a regular pick-up point. Simultaneously a patrol of about 10 men walked along the far bank of the river hiding themselves carefully.

At the next stop, two militants carrying weapon boarded the boat and demanded money. NJ, who could speak the local language, asked them to surrender. Not complying with the demand, one of the militants standing close to NJ brought out his weapon and was ready to shoot him. But NJ was quicker. He drew his pistol and shot at the militant through his jaw. The second militant however fired at NJ. The bullet passed through his thighs. After firing, the second militant jumped into water. With total disregard to his injury and bleeding, NJ jumped into the river and went after the militant. With the help of the other men walking along the far bank, the second militant was apprehended. Thus both militants were accounted for.

NJ had lost a lot blood. His condition became serious. He was evacuated for medical treatment. After a long and competent medical treatment by some of the best surgeons, he recovered fully.

For this act of courage, ingenious method of operation and devotion to duty of a high order, Major NJ Nair was awarded the KIRTI CHAKRA (KC), the second highest award in the Indian Army for the act of bravery outside the battle field (i.e. when war is not declared; an insurgent is not termed as enemy).

After this operation, Mizo militants stopped using the river. The local population was grateful to NJ and they became very supportive of the Army operations. Denial of the use of the river, extensive presence of the Army and loss of major source of their income had forced the insurgents to move out of this area.

Colonel NJ Nair KC, was appointed as Commanding Officer of 16 MLI when the unit was stationed at Chennai on August 7, 1992. It is a dream for Infantry officers 'to command the battalion in which he was commissioned'. From Chennai, the Battalion moved to yet another insurgency prone area; this time Nagaland. With his previous experience in Mizoram and having been an instructor at the Intelligence School, the Battalion could not have found a more suitable Commanding Officer to lead the unit in their future assignment.

During his tenure as Commanding Officer, the Battalion had launched many successful operations against Naga underground militants and established dominance in their area of responsibility. The rumors were afloat that Naga underground leaders went dormant during NJ's tenure in his area of responsibility and were waiting for NJ to leave Nagaland. However, the subsequent events prove this wrong.

In December 1993, after having operated away from the Base for quite some time, the Battalion was returning to their Base. Movement in large convoys through Road Mokokchung - Mariani is not without danger. Numerous sharp curves in this stretch of road slow down the speed of the convoys and present attractive targets for militants to ambush. Arranging protection against such threats at every suspected place is not practicable. Hence, security is provided selectively.

On 20 December, NJ left the unit area at about 4.30 AM with his protection party to reach Jorhat ahead of the rest of the Battalion so that en-route, he could visit his men who were admitted in the Military Hospital.

At about 8 AM, when the vehicles were negotiating a road bent, NJ's convoy came under heavy automatic fire from many places. In the initial volley of fire, 14 men died and many were injured. NJ himself was injured. With indomitable courage and total disregard to his personal safety, NJ decided to avenge the loss of his men and organized his protection party to break the ambush. He asked one of his men to climb over his shoulder for better visibility and lob grenades at the militants. This deterred the militants from further firing accurately.

Thereafter, with his men he charged at the ambush site, killed one militant, and injured a few others. The militants ran away and escaped into the jungle. NJ, along with a few men, chased the militants. With the advantage of the cover provided by the terrain, the militants vanished in the jungle. NJ became a martyr (for heroes like NJ never die). His body was found about 300 ms from the road, inside the jungle.

For this act of iron will, raw courage and bold determination to fight till the end, Colonel NJ Nair KC, was awarded ASHOK CHAKRA (AC); the highest award for bravery outside the battlefield.

Thus, NJ has risen to the pedestal of the **Bravest of the Braves**. He is unique in the annals of the Indian Army, who has been awarded both ASHOK CHAKRA and KIRTI CHAKRA. His contribution to the laurels of the MARATHA LIGHT INFANTRY will remain etched in golden letters and add to the rich history of His Regiment and the history of Indian Army.

Memorials have been erected at all organizations where he was trained or served to remind the future generations that NJ was the **Bravest of Braves**. Main Office Building at MLI Training Centre and Lobby at NDAs main office have been named after him. NJ lives through these memorials to inspire the Bold and Fearless.

PEACEKEEPING OPERATIONS

Since Independence, India has taken active part in United Nations sponsored peace keeping and peace enforcing operations in many countries and earned meritorious citations.

The first commitment of our units after independence was in Korea. Lt Col Dr Ranga Raj; a World War II veteran was awarded a Maha Vir Chakra for carrying out many life saving surgeries. In July 1953 Lt Gen KS Thimayya was appointed as the Chairman of UN Prisoners Repatriation Commission. The Indians earned the respect of UN Forces as well as the opposing Communist Forces.

Indian Army Units were employed in Congo to prevent the warring groups from destroying the nation. At times our troops had to fight pitched battles in their effort to keep peace. Capt GS Salaria of 3/1 GR was awarded PVC posthumously. In addition, three MVC and 20 VrCs were also awarded.

4 J&K Rifles defeated a strong ambush set by the Khmer Rouge in Cambodia. The unit earned one Kirti Chakra and two Sena medals. The CO, Col AN Bahuguna was awarded YSM.

In addition to the above, Indian Contingents participated in the operations in Gaza, Somalia, Rwanda, Mozambique and Angola. Nearer home, the Indian Peace Keeping Operations in Srilanka involved battling back and forth in jungles, towns and lagoons and paid very heavy price to maintain peace there. Maj Parameswarn of 8 Mahar was awarded PVC(posthumous) for successfully clearing an ambush. The quick response to the call of Maldives saved the life of their President and normalcy was restored within a week.

Our performance in the UN peace Keeping Operations have been of a very high order. It has earned the respect and admiration of other armies of the world.

KIPPER AND SAM THE HISTORY MAKERS

Amongst the history makers of the Indian Army, two legendary soldiers stand tall. Not only because both them had reached the pinnacle in the rank structure and stature in our Army, but also they were true soldier of soldiers. They were Field marshals until they breathed last in their mid-nineties. One of them had laid a strong foundation to the newly born Indian Army and set standards for a first class Army and the other lead that Army to an indisputable victory before the Indian Army celebrated it's silver jubilee.

Elder of the two, Kodandera Madappa Cariappa was born in Coorg District of present day Karnataka on 28 January 1899. After his education at Coorg and Presidency College Chennai, he was selected for the first batch of Indians for Kings Commission. He underwent his pre-commission training in UK before he was commissioned into Carnatic Infantry as 2/Lt. Later he joined the Rajput Regiment. He was one the first batch students to attend Staff Course at Quetta. He saw the World War II in Iran/Iraq and then in the Slim's 10th Army. He was the first Indian Officer to Command an Infantry Battalion.

By 1947, he had attended a higher warfare course in UK and become a Major General. During the Indo - Pak partition he was one of the officer responsible to divide the assets of the British Indian Army into two. This delicate job was done in a most amicable manner. After the Independence, he was initially appointed as the Eastern Army Commander and later shifted to Western Army during the First Kashmir War.

His patriotism did not permit him to toe the lines of the Commander in Chief (C in C) of India General Butcher, but he followed what was best in the interest of his motherland. He used to say that for him there are only two Stans; Hindustan and Fauzistan. He greatly contributed to the victory of Indian Army in the first Kashmir war that Indian Army fought immediately after independence and in the consolidation of Indian Princely States.

He was elevated to the rank of General and became the first Indian C in C of the Army replacing General Butcher. There is an interesting anecdote about his appointment as Commander in Chief. The Indian Govt headed by

Nehru had decided to relieve General Butcher of his position as C in C and a suitable foreigner was being considered since Nehru thought that Indian Army Officers did not have the experience of Commanding an Army. Lt Gen Nathu Singh Rathore who attended a meeting with Nehru and his cabinet heard this and suggested that in that case India should also look for an experienced Prime Minister as India did not have one. On this the Prime Minister asked Lt Gen Nathu Singh whether he was ready take over as the C in C. Nathu answered 'I know someone who is more suitable than me for that post'; he was Lt Gen KM Cariappa. This is how Cariappa became a General and the first Indian C in C on 15 January 1949 and later first Chief of the Army Staff on 15 January 1950 and remained until 1953.

During this period, he ensured that the Indian Army is well organized, trained, motivated and has strong regimentation. He is responsible for adding the Brigade of Guards and Parachute Regiment with All India Class composition to the list of Infantry Regiments. It was during his time the National Cadet Corps and Territorial Army was raised. Well being of the Army and its morale was always close to his heart. He was a visionary who lived by the ideals of a soldier and leader. He is instrumental in converting the British Indian Army into truly an Indian Army. He emphasized on the need for industrial growth along with the armed forces for the defense of the nation. His secular outlook manifested in all walks of Indian Army.

Later he was appointed as our High Commissioner to Australia and Newziland. He was presented with the 'Order of the Chief Commander of the Legion of Merit' by Hary Truman the then US President. On 14 January 1986 he was honored with the Rank of Field Marshal for his contribution to our Nation Building.

FM KM Cariappa

During the wars that Indian Army fought after he left his active service, he used to visit troops in the forward areas to boast their morale. He always carried and distributed small gifts to all those whom he met. Immaculately turned out he used to mingle with men and be at ease with them. He believed in patriotism and secularism and lived by it until he passed away on 15 May 1993. The beautiful memorial at Medicari, Coorg reminds the visitors of the greatness this soldier had achieved in his life of 94 years.

The second legendary soldier and a prominent history maker of the Indian Army was born at Amritsar on 03 April 1914. Manekshaw, after his college studies at Sherwood College Nainital was commissioned from the Indian Military Academy Dehradun into the 2nd Battalion of Royal Scots and later served with 12 Frontier Force. During the World War II as a capt, he led his company to a successful attack against Japanese post in Burma. He was severely wounded during the attack. Seeing his serious condition and suspecting that he may not survive, Major General Goven who was impressed by the brilliant leadership and bravery of the Young Captain on the face of the enemy, pinned his own Military Cross on Capt Manekshaw.

He was evacuated for treatment. The surgeon who examined him asked him what had happened. Sam told him, "I was kicked by a bloody mule." The surgeon laughed and said "Given your sense of humor, it will be worth saving you!" He underwent a series of successful operations and was saved. Back in India after some rest and recouperation, he was detailed to attend the staff course at Quetta.

Later he was selected by Field Marshal Auchinlek to go on a lecture tour to Australia with a view to project the image of the Indian Army. After independence, he was transferred to 5 Gorkha Rifles and was designated to command the 3rd Battalion of 5 GR though he never commanded the Battalion. During 1947 War, while serving at the Army Headquarters, he worked closely with the Defense Ministers and had a lot of exposure to higher level decision making and politics.

He commanded a Brigade and later a Division successfully. He was selected as the Colonel of the 8 GR. He was commandant of the Defense Services Staff College Wellington. Later in 1962, he was given the command of 4 Corps during Chinese Aggression. On assuming command of the retreating Corps, he had issued an order that there will be no withdrawal without written orders and these orders shall never be issued.

In November 1963 he was appointed as the Western Army Commander and later to Eastern Army. On 8 June 1969, General Sam Manekshaw took over as 8th Chief of the Army. In April 1971, Govt of India had decided to solve the refugee problem from East Pakistan by military intervention. The Chief was asked to liberate East Pakistan immediately. Sam refused to rush his Army and suffer a defeat. He asked for time to prepare for the war and promised victory.

Prime Minister Mrs Indira Gandhi was not happy in spite of the valid and strategically sound reasoning advanced by Sam. Sam had offered to resign. He practiced what he preached that a 'yesman' is a dangerous man. Govt ultimately relented and accepted Sam's plan.

With the intimate co-operation with Navy and Air force, a plan was conceived by which Pakistani Forces in the East were to be forced to surrender enmass and as quickly as possible. Sam chose the best campaigning season that is December after considering various factors including climatic conditions and adequate time to make up the weapon and equipment profile and prepare for the war thoroughly.

The war when launched, lasted less than 15 days and Pakistan Army in the East surrendered with nearly one lakh PsOW taken at the end of War. A new country, Bangladesh was born. Sam was awarded Padma Vibhushan for his service to the nation. Every year on 16 December, Vijay Diwas in memory of the victory achieved under Manekshaw's leadership in 1971 is celebrated.

FM Sam Bahadur

On 01 January 1973 he was honored with the rank of Field Marshal, the first Indian Field Marshal and on 15 January, he relinquished the active service. In recognition to his love of Gorkha Soldier, Nepal Govt made him honorary General of their Army. He is known to have said, "If a man says he is not afraid of dying, he is either lying or is a Gurkha".

After 25 more years of his busy life, he died on 27 June 2008. On his death Barak Obama the present President of USA said,"I offer my deep condolences to the people of India, on the passing of Field Marshal Sam Manekshaw. He was a legendary soldier, a patriot, and an inspiration to his fellow citizens,"

Kipper and Sam Bahadur as they were known, provided an example of personal bravery, self sacrifice, and steadfast devotion to duty. No doubt they were soldiers par excellence with courage of conviction. Their memory will be cherished as the History Makers.

www.ingramcontent.com/pod-product-compliance
Lightning Source LLC
Chambersburg PA
CBHW070920180426
43192CB00038B/1986